UNIVERSITY PARTNERSHIP PLAYBOOK

UNIVERSITY PARTNERSHIP PLAYBOOK

How to Build Strategic Research Relationships

MATT REED AND JOSS LANGFORD

LIVERPOOL UNIVERSITY PRESS

First published 2021 by
Liverpool University Press
4 Cambridge Street
Liverpool
L69 7ZU

British Library Cataloguing-in-Publication data
A British Library CIP record is available

ISBN 978-1-78962-126-6

Typeset by Carnegie Book Production, Lancaster
Printed and bound by CPI Group (UK) Ltd, Croydon CR0 4YY

CONTENTS

LIST OF FIGURES

LIST OF TABLES

I.
PREFACE

This playbook provides guidance to commercial innovators on how best to exploit the knowledge and resource capital of universities. It has been written by practitioners, for practitioners. It will help you to develop a more strategic approach to building relationships with a university or other academic institution. It will enhance the research, innovation, and product development capabilities of the company you work for. If you use the tools we present here, you will be able to form productive and long-lasting partnerships that will benefit both your company and your collaborators.

A playbook works by describing set pieces and well-known 'plays'. It is a term that originated in North America to describe and catalogue sporting tactics, but it has now been adopted into business practice. In this instance, the 'plays' we focus on are those that typically occur or need to be navigated when working with a university. A playbook sets out a menu of tips and tools, but it still requires that you improvise, use, and improve the tools that we present. This is not a step-by-step instruction manual.

The first edition of this book arose from the needs of a specific corporation, Unilever, at a specific time – from about 2008 to 2019. It reflected the needs of Unilever as they developed an Open Innovation strategy with a strong emphasis on university partnering. Unilever had spent a lot of money and resources on university partnerships in a long period running up to about 2010. After that, it made a conscious move towards spending less in cash terms, but with high expectations of impact. It was able to achieve this because of the high degree of retained in-house knowledge on partnerships and a strategic shift to open innovation ecosystems.

The main change we, as authors, have made for this edition of the playbook is to alter our tone of voice. In the first edition it was implicit that 'we' meant a team of Unilever research and innovation leaders who needed to create and manage university partnerships. In this edition, this is no longer the case. 'We' now refers to the co-authors, Matt and Joss. 'You' is a reader who wants to understand from a company perspective how to develop a strategic approach for your business to access early-stage research.

In creating this second edition we have made some changes, mainly to ensure that the work is relevant to commercial organisations other than Unilever. We have also stretched the scope in a couple of directions. We believe that large organisations with a different experience than Unilever's will be interested in reading the book, and that it will also be valuable to smaller organisations that have less money and high expectations, with varying amounts of partnership management experience.

We believe that the playbook could be important for many types of organisation and we have modified the content to capture this. As well as needing to consider a wider type of organisation, we have taken the opportunity to address a much broader range of readers. The original book was intended for a commercial research and innovation audience. In this edition, we make sure that a larger audience can benefit from it – for example, an MBA student working on a project about academic partnering, or someone working in the procurement function of a large pharma business.

One of the reasons we wrote the playbook, and the particular form we have given it, reflects our own experience and that of others that there is a gap in the market for this material. The topic has been explored before by authors, but not as presented here, with succinct sections, originality, and useful references. Compared to other lengthier published materials, we hope this playbook leads readers to a level of understanding that will allow them to explore and try new approaches of collaboration with confidence. We have aimed to simplify the complexity of engaging with universities and provide practical illustrations that will be of immediate help to relationship managers in companies and universities.

You should be able to read this book from cover to cover in a few hours. However, we hope you will be motivated to return to the book from time to time as you begin to use the tools, frameworks, and templates as part of your ongoing partnering work.

2.
INTRODUCTION

Research and development (R&D) continues to be at the heart of how businesses and governments realise technological potential and foster innovation. But the way R&D is conducted today is changing rapidly. Knowledge ecosystems are shifting towards cross-disciplinary, multi-agency activities that draw on the distinct contributions that different types of organisation can make towards developing and exploiting original and transformative ideas. We are also seeing a growing trend and need for international collaboration, alongside the emergence of clusters of elite research groups working collaboratively with each other.

Although commercial organisations have long understood the role that universities can play as concentrated hotspots of knowledge and talent, the increasing development of the modern knowledge-intensive economy has further highlighted their importance. The fundamental reason why companies are looking to partner more strongly with universities is that they are becoming vital 'knowledge platforms' – with new responsibilities as key stakeholders in the leadership and development of research and innovation that can create new business, address profound societal challenges, and support industrial transformations. This playbook addresses this why, as well as the how.

Across the globe, engagements between universities and companies happen every day. They range in scale from short-term studentships to substantial multi-year co-investments. Often universities will host visiting researchers from companies or will develop networks that help students find work. Some engagements are short and transactional, others may last over decades. There are many forms of company–university engagement, and no two collaborations are the same. There are many different types of experience you will have with university partnerships, and for that reason outcomes may vary. Given these points, we believe there is no single process; the book therefore provides an overview of the various facets of company–university collaboration and provides support for successfully navigating the issues you will need to address in practice.

If you have picked up this playbook, then it is likely that you will have some questions such as these:

- How do you create alignment around your research needs?
- How do you effectively scout a university for opportunities and talent?
- How do you create social capital in a university relationship?
- How do you exploit the social capital captured in a university relationship?
- How do you work with partners to leverage further resources?
- What structures are needed to maintain effective partnerships?
- How do you manage risk with universities?
- What attributes and skills do you and your team need to maintain, navigate, and strengthen relationships?

The tools we present have been developed to cover all these questions and more – from how you manage individual-to-individual relationships to build trust and understanding, through to how you assess the partnership potential of a department against your core business needs. They will help you to define a problem in terms that are interesting to a university researcher and establish agreements that provide ongoing access to the knowledge, capabilities, and services that meet the requirements of all partners.

There is increasing pressure from governments to ensure that good ideas don't become orphaned at a discovery or invention phase of development. Stakeholders understand they have an obligation to try and ensure that the best ideas find a way to create an impact through application. Companies need to bring new technologies to market with agile and responsive processes that can help organisations respond to changing consumer and customer trends, including widespread changes in societal demands such as environmental sustainability. We are finding that high-quality research partnerships are fostered through mutually beneficial arrangements between research leaders, placing greater onus on academic institutions to create the conditions for collaboration.

Traditionally, throughout the nineteenth and twentieth centuries, the impact arising from university research in the natural sciences was through the education and development of individuals, and through the publication and dissemination of peer-reviewed papers, books, and monographs. Much of the knowledge transfer from leading researchers to more junior staff, and thence to industry, was enacted through PhD training – which was effectively an apprenticeship in research technique.

Impact has now increased in importance, and additional routes to impact have become common. In the twenty-first century, impact from university research routinely arises from:

- People (human capital development through PhD and postdoctoral activity).
- Publications (knowledge development and dissemination through papers, books, and monographs).
- Patents (discrete commercial opportunities through licences and/or spin-outs of inventions).
- Policy (guiding government through influential networks).

In some academic fields, such as statistics, open-source software has become a key route to impact, for example the Comprehensive R Archive (https://cran.r-project.org/). But there is an even newer, and much more powerful route to impact for economic, academic, and societal benefits – the concept of platforms. These are digital assets accessed via programming interfaces (known as APIs) that allow users to benefit from specialised scientific and technical knowledge, anywhere in the world, and at any time.

To date, the systematic creation and exploitation of platforms from world-class research in most universities is in its infancy. We note that properly engineered platforms not only create new impact opportunities, they also have a positive feedback effect on the pace and quality of research in the core research groups.

Organisations are consciously building *ecosystems* that include local and regional relationships, alongside global networks that coalesce around world-leading knowledge, shared values, and interests. The majority of multinational R&D teams will find themselves operating across enormous geographic scales. Even within the same corporation, researchers will often be in labs separated by hundreds or thousands of kilometres. It is commonplace for big corporate R&D organisations to have labs in the US, Europe, India, and China.

The most forward-looking corporations know that their external academic partnerships not only deliver commercial benefits to their shareholders, but that they also deliver outstanding impact to the institutions themselves, their communities, and students by working together on high-quality applied science and technology. Good company–academic relationships can *do good*, by doing great science. The best of these partnerships lead to the co-creation of long-term sustainable capability, assets, and knowledge across a wide range of relevant disciplines, all of which are brought to bear on problems worth solving.

We have found that company–academic relationships can only flourish when there is openness, integrity, and trust between partners who have a shared pragmatism and passion for science and innovation that matters. Wherever a good company–university partnership is found, you will find great relationship managers, people who have learnt that close knowledge partnerships are built up over time and are 'human led', rather than 'contract led'. Individual projects get the attention they deserve and often more attention than the overall costs would suggest.

The role of a research or innovation leader in a company has changed significantly in the past two decades. While leadership in R&D comes in different flavours, the highest-impact leaders are now expected to blend programme leadership, people leadership, and thought leadership. These are just a few of the new demands on researchers, research leaders, and senior managers in companies and in universities.

Business life is even more demanding and complex than it used to be. Historically, it was what an R&D leader knew themselves that drove performance and generated value. Today, on top of what you know, your intellectual and technical abilities, you are called upon to use a wide range of additional skills and attributes. These may be used to help you mobilise knowledge and people, promote collaborative working, and foster innovation. The ability to use these skills and resources strategically is central to achieving successful access to early-stage research.

A strategic partnership is perhaps the deepest form of relationship that can exist across two organisations while both parties still retain their individual autonomy and identity. Strategic partnerships typically consist of an agreement between two organisations, stipulating arrangements for ongoing access to resources, workspaces, knowledge sharing, and skills exchanges. They will be underpinned by reciprocity, enabling each partner to share specific areas of strength with the other, thereby generating a value exchange that is more than the sum of its parts, and a shared commitment to the partnership. For the partnership to endure, it must be vital to the core business needs of each partner. Investments and risks are shared and navigated cooperatively for mutual gain.

The benefits of an appropriately aligned strategic partnership are many-fold. They enable conversations and joint planning based on knowledge of one another's strengths and gaps. They help reduce transaction costs associated with project-by-project working, reducing set-up times and legal overheads. They bring additional resources and capabilities into play that can bear directly on key business challenges. They open the possibilities of co-investment in strategic capabilities, and for co-branding opportunities, which can then be used as leverage for additional investments and impact. Finally, organisations can exert greater influence when working together in alignment.

A term that we will use throughout this playbook is *social capital*. This is a valuable commodity that is shared across the parties in a partnership; it can be accrued or depleted over time, but is ultimately the sum total of the knowledge, attitudes, networks, values, and resources that are nested within the web of relationships.

In recognition of the benefits of strategic partnering, many world-leading multinationals are changing the nature of their academic relationships. The increasing emphasis on a handful of partners means that the companies can aim higher, focus on enriching these partnerships, and leverage more value from them. Prioritisation is necessary, as it is simply not possible to run dozens of strategic partnerships because of the time and resources that are needed to develop and maintain them. Moving from an ad hoc relationship to a strategic partnership requires a shift in how you think about partnering.

3.
THE SET-UP

Before you develop your approach to university partnerships, you will already have a beginning level of confidence and competence at managing this sort of relationship. We believe it is important that you take time to ground yourself, by understanding where you currently are, before trying to articulate where you want to get to. Levels of maturity change over time, based on learning, experience of good and bad project outcomes, and changes in the strategic context in which you work.

In order to guide you, we have developed a simple five-level maturity model – shown in Table 1. We believe that this is self-explanatory. It is framed in terms of individual behaviours, so it can be applied to an individual's own development, but it can also be read as an organisational level of maturity.

MATURITY LEVEL	TYPICAL BEHAVIOUR AND MINDSET OF INDIVIDUAL OR ORGANISATION
1	Rarely considers looking for knowledge assets outside their own company. Assumes that the time and effort needed to create a partnership is much more than learning how to do something oneself.
2	Has identified an attractive source of university knowledge, but lacks experience of how to structure an interaction and proceeds warily.
3	Routinely enters into small-scale ad hoc projects with individual academics at one or more universities. May rely on own academic experience as the main route to opening opportunities.
4	Has established a range of good-quality relationships with both individual university academics and research teams. Routinely exploits early-stage research as part of a wider innovation strategy. Understands an academic partner in the wider context of funding bodies, spin-outs, and intermediaries.
5	Shows a sophisticated understanding of how to structure and exploit multi-agency and multi-year partnerships with academic institutions. By default looks for knowledge assets outside their own company. Understands exactly what their company can do better than external partners, but also understands how to seamlessly integrate external expertise into company activities.

Table 1: Levels of organisational maturity in university partnering.

4.
DIGITAL

As a consequence of the worldwide COVID crisis in 2020, the CEO of Microsoft, Satya Nadella, concluded in April 2020 that 'We saw two years of digital transformation in two months'. Digital technologies are helping us to find new ways of working together, enabling easier access and sharing of knowledge. They are also transforming how R&D and commercial innovation are done. They open new ways to exploit and connect innovation assets (such as people, knowledge, and resources) and change the ways in which they can create value. They are helping us to bring different players within an ecosystem closer, recognising their organisational cultures and practices, building trust and relationship capital, and establishing new ways of doing things together.

Digital technologies give us new ways to overcome traditional barriers to innovation such as the physical time and space that different players occupy. The technologies provide opportunities for teams who are remote from physical assets to both benefit from them and to help drive their development. Ultimately, they are helping us to better exploit the world's collective brainpower and connect us with the world-leading expertise of specific individuals.

In some important ways, it is becoming clear that the only truly global knowledge assets are those that have already been digitised:

- Their marginal cost of replication and movement is zero.
- They move at the speed of light.
- They are available simultaneously in all time zones across the globe.

But digital is not inhuman. It is roughly one-third software, one-third hardware, and one-third peopleware (DeMarco and Lister 1999). And in all three cases, it is highly skilled people who remain vital in the development and use of digital platforms. This includes productivity, how people collaborate, and how people learn to use systems. Even a digitally enabled innovation ecosystem still needs people and equipment on the ground.

5.
RISK AND UNCERTAINTY

Research and innovation by their nature involve *uncertainty*: there are many possible outcomes from a particular activity or programme. By definition, if an outcome was 100% predictable, it would not be research. But uncertainty does not always imply risk. An uncertainty only becomes a risk when one or more of the possible outcomes would lead to an unwanted event, a major loss, large downside, or other undesirable effect. Many commercial organisations will accept that many, if not all, of their innovation activities have uncertain outcomes. But they are generally unhappy to commit significant resources to uncertain outcomes that also represent appreciable risks.

Risk assessment methods generally distinguish between the two types of measure that a company, project, or team can apply to a given situation. There are *control measures*, which are designed to prevent an unwanted event occurring in the first place, and *mitigation measures*, which are designed to limit the adverse consequences of an unwanted event if it occurs. The analysis usually tries to quantify the outstanding risk in the presence of these control and mitigation measures.

Some companies see external innovation collaborations as not only embodying uncertainty, but also as a source of risk. By avoiding an external collaboration, they feel that this also minimises their risks. Here, the control measure they are applying is to avoid the collaboration with a university. Alternatively, they go ahead with the collaboration, but take extraordinary care with their legal team to mitigate any and all of the possible downsides through extensive and complex legal agreements. Unfortunately, these control and mitigation measures not only insulate the company from downside risks, they also ensure that the company doesn't get the chance to benefit from the very large potential upside of an external collaboration with the first-rate knowledge assets they can find in a university. While you are unlikely to be able to radically change the risk response of your organisation, recognising its maturity level will help you to identify incremental changes that will better support new partnerships.

We have found that in many complex situations with uncertain outcomes, surprisingly simple tools can often work better than more complicated and rigid rules, regulations, control measures, and legal constructs. It is this approach that we apply throughout this book – the tools and techniques presented here help you to make decisions under uncertainty. This approach ultimately derives from the work of Herbert A. Simon (1916–2001), who won the Nobel prize in economics in 1978. One of Simon's most stimulating ideas was his theory of *satisficing*. This word is a blend of satisfy and suffice. It means: 'To decide on and pursue a course of action that will satisfy the minimum requirements necessary to achieve a particular goal' (Simon 1947). This approach has been extended by many others, most notably perhaps Gerd Gigerenzer (for example, see Gigerenzer 2015). As Andrew Haldane, Chief Economist at the Bank of England points out:

> Under risk, policy should respond to every raindrop; it is fine-tuned. Under uncertainty, that logic is reversed. Complex environments often instead call for simple decision rules. That is because these rules are more robust to ignorance. Under uncertainty, policy may only respond to every thunderstorm; it is coarse-tuned.

> (Haldane and Madouros 2012)

It is in dynamic situations, when decisions are inevitably made under uncertainty, that a playbook helps the most. The resources presented in this book will help you in two ways. For complex situations, we present some tools to help you *divide and conquer* – so that when broken down into smaller blocks, you can more easily make sense of a situation and manage it. Other tools are designed to help reveal some of the layers of complexity that can be hidden within apparently simple scenarios.

6.
UNDERSTANDING
A UNIVERSITY

You will soon find that each and every university you engage with or work with will be different. They each have a specific history, focus, and culture, and they all have slightly different ways of working. In this section we explore some of the common characteristics and idiosyncrasies of universities and other academic institutions. We will begin to unpack their core purpose, their mission, what you can and can't reasonably expect from them. We will also help you to look beyond the corporate structures in the university towards building partnerships that can directly harness research and knowledge capabilities.

Universities are full of brilliant people and by design they strive to work at the forefront of scientific discovery and invention. Globally, universities benefit from generous state support for their research and development activities, alongside a steady income from tuition fees. This comparatively secure funding for research enables universities to maintain and develop their research programmes and capabilities across a broad spectrum of scientific disciplines.

Compared to commercial research and development organisations, universities are more able to invest in long-term and high-risk scientific research across a much broader palette of subjects. While no two universities are exactly the same, there are some general characteristics that are worth knowing to help you understand them. To begin with, all universities and academic institutions have three priorities:

- *Educating future leaders and citizens.* Providing outstanding learning and life experiences for their students so they graduate with robust intellectual capabilities, employability, leadership qualities, and the ability to contribute to society.
- *Pushing at the boundaries of knowledge.* Striving beyond the current state of the art in human knowledge through scholarship and research, and widely disseminating the results of this activity in peer-reviewed journals, magazines, monographs, books, conferences, and seminars.
- *Speaking truth to power.* Using their non-commercial and independent position to help ensure that civil society has access to a wide range of challenging and independent views on the world – in politics, economics, ethics, science, environment, and technology.

If you are looking to partner with the best universities, to gain access to world-leading knowledge, graduates, and capabilities, it is vital to be able to differentiate between different types of university so that you can engage with those that match your needs and ambitions. You will most likely already know within your context which universities are world leading, but as a rule of thumb you should be looking for evidence of:

- A high concentration or critical mass of talent in both the permanent faculty and the student body.
- Sufficient resources to provide extensive, comprehensive learning conditions and a rich environment for advanced research.
- Favourable governance allowing and encouraging autonomy, strategic vision, innovation, efficient resource management, and flexibility.

There are several university ranking systems to which you can refer. They all require some interpretation and should be taken as just one of several sources of information as you often need to drill down to the credentials of the faculty you are working with. The Times Higher Education World University Rankings is one that looks across core missions – teaching, research, knowledge transfer, and international outlook; another is the QS World University Rankings.

7.
BUILDING A PEN PORTRAIT

Many years of partnering experience have shown us that creating significant output from university research requires explicit attention to the creation of alignment with the people, resources, and capabilities that lie below the surface and beyond the corporate legal agreements. It is important when working in a close partnership to build a good understanding of the working culture and values of the institution you are working with.

We have found that you cannot do this well without first understanding the fundamental differences between university research and commercial R&D. There is no need for a formal framework for this, but we have found a number of key prompts that help to develop a pen portrait. This is useful ammunition to take into conversations with different stakeholders, some of whom will have little interest in the technical content of your partnership. These prompts serve to highlight that each university will be proud of its specific history, governance, and legacy, and coming into conversations aware of this will help you to build trust and social capital, and raise the esteem in which your company is held as a viable partner.

ASPECT	QUESTION
History	How and why was it founded? When was it founded?
Size and structure	What is the size and scale of the institution? How is the institution organised (faculties, etc.)?
What is it famous for?	What key science and technology has the institution contributed to (in any field)?
Location and reach	Where are the local, regional, global, and satellite sites? Where are any key partners located?
Other collaborations	What are the institution's other key alliances with industry, competitors, and other partners? How successful were these projects?
Capability areas	What capability areas are already known? What else might you be interested in?
Unique sales points	What are the institution's valuable differentiators in relation to other institutions?
Quality of academic body	Who and where are the strong players/groups? Which (if any) groups should be avoided?
Non-academics	How professional, experienced, and commercially minded are teams such as the contracts office? How well do they understand your challenges?
Exemplar projects	What is your company's track record with the university in terms of investment and success?

Table 2: Prompts to help you build a pen portrait of a university.

8.
THE ICEBERG MODEL

A university is much like an iceberg, where most of its people and resources lie underneath the surface. The tip of the iceberg, the part that you can see easily, is the corporate leadership of the university and their supporting professional services team. These elements include the university council, rector, vice-chancellor, faculty leadership, contracts office, technology transfer office, and so on. It is relatively easy for most organisations to see a university at this level, and for many universities, the corporate leadership will be actively looking to engage with medium and large companies. But from our experience, even though engagement with this part of the university might lead to a memorandum of understanding and/or a statement of intent, it is only when working with the nine-tenths of the workforce that are labouring away below the surface, employed in research, teaching, and scholarship, that any appreciable delivery and impact can be achieved.

Figure 1: The university as an iceberg.

There is only a loose coupling between the corporate part of the university and individual researchers and departments. Researchers will most likely identify themselves first with their discipline and subject specialism, prior to any identification with the institution in which they are based. Obtaining value from the 90% is therefore about developing alignment with the individual researchers, investigators, and expertise leaders. Aligning with the tip of the iceberg is straightforward; this playbook is about partnering both *above* and *below* the waterline.

If you can develop a healthy and dynamic partnership, this will help you to create an effective open and collaborative way of doing business, which is essentially borderless, and is not bound by existing internal R&D staff alone. This capacity can be applied to build emerging science areas, and also to supplement in-house capability for more mature science areas. In some cases, it can help to lower full-time employee (FTE) costs or accelerate the impact of other investments.

9.
ECOSYSTEM INNOVATION

This chapter and the following one describe how university partnerships fit into a larger idea of 'innovation ecosystems'. We introduce the concept of an innovation ecosystem and will help you to understand the positions and roles a commercial organisation can play within these ecosystems. The following chapter describes how you can place your own company, how it innovates and operates, within an ecosystem that includes a university partner as a key contributor to that ecosystem.

We see university partnerships as part of larger ecosystems in which invention and innovation operate. Innovation and technology development are often the result of a complex set of relationships among entrepreneurs, companies, universities, research organisations, investors, and government agencies. 'Innovation ecosystem' is a term that has become widely used to describe the dynamic and interdependent network that exists between these agents to generate, diffuse, and create value. An innovation ecosystem can be defined as 'a dynamic interdependent network of agents interacting in a specific economic/industrial field with the explicit aim to generate, diffuse, and create value from technology and its utilization' (adapted from Carlsson and Stankiewicz 1991).

Underpinning an ecosystem is a set of interactions and relationships that represent social capital, the totality of knowledge, attitudes, networks, values, and resources held within these relationships. In common with financial capital, social capital can be created through investment, harvested for value through careful exploitation, and wasted through inexpert or clumsy management. There are a number of aspects that constitute and make up social capital:

- *Human* – people, skills, person-to-person networks, knowledge.
- *Structural* – companies, organisations, programmes, infrastructure.
- *Interrelational* – trust, confidence, shared vision, coherent behaviours, culture.

It is important to understand both who is involved in an innovation process and how they are involved. To build strategic partnerships within innovation ecosystems, you must examine the nature of the relationships that need to exist between people, enterprises, and institutions for innovation to flourish.

A thriving ecosystem will enable *all actors in the ecosystem* to interact effectively to strengthen the impact and potential of their research and development activities. Innovation ecosystems function well when they embody some operating principles. These principles may emerge in an arbitrary way as an ecosystem is formed, or they may be explicitly articulated, codified, and agreed before and during the creation of the ecosystem. These principles will dictate who is active in the ecosystem and who is not. They might also set out and codify the ways of working within the system, often focusing on concepts of openness, trust, sharing, and conflict resolution, for example.

For an ecosystem to remain dynamic and flexible, it needs to be able to absorb significant changes in its overall shape and size while remaining viable. Good innovation ecosystems manage to remain porous to new capital, new partnerships, and new ways of working. They are not overly constrained by jurisdictional boundaries or geographies, nor are they overly reliant on formal structures. The real focus for innovators working to build ecosystems has to be on the quality of interactions within and between the structures and actors in their ecosystem.

Working within an innovation ecosystem will require you to shift your mindset away from traditional ways of working and doing business. You must bring into focus how you can create opportunities for people to work together effectively in different ways to unlock creativity and innovation. You will need to create an environment that fosters sharing, the perusal of opportunities and options, and curiosity and trust. Command and control strategies need to be avoided. It is vital to seek a wider recognition of how social capital is built, using organisational and individual learning as a key driver for improvement, adoption, and innovation.

This change in mindset then needs to flow into an evolution in the language you use in partnership. Perceptions of business challenges are informed by the language used to describe problems. In traditional ways of working, the language will typically highlight ownership (e.g. intellectual property) or known outcomes; in innovation ecosystems, the language shifts onto emergent outcomes, shared risk, and shared access. At the highest level, the shift required is from a set of assumptions based on a *command and control* mindset, to assumptions based on *sharing and access*. The need for these shifts is well recognised (Doz and Hamel 1998) and they are illustrated across a range of business and innovation dimensions in Table 3. For example, a command-and-control mindset will lead to targets being based on already known or expected outcomes. In contrast, an ecosystem mindset will retain a set of expected outcomes, but will also enthusiastically embrace and exploit opportunities that emerge from the activities of the ecosystem. At an individual level, an ecosystem innovator spends less time trying to be the inventor, and more time orchestrating the invention and innovation activities of a network of people who don't work in their organisation.

FROM	DIMENSION	TO
Binary negotiations	**Negotiating**	Multiple-player deals
Owning resources	**Resources**	Accessing shared resources
Targeting known outcomes	**Outcomes**	Embracing emergence
Minimising and avoiding risk	**Risk**	Sharing risk
All of a small pie	**Control**	Sharing a big pie
Inventor	**Innovation**	Innovation orchestrator
Pure science	**Science**	Applied science
Our laboratory	**Facilities**	Technology landscapes
Linear	**Relationships**	Networked
Convergence	**Thinking style**	Divergence
Tightrope walking	**Management**	Plate spinning

Table 3: Shifting mindsets for innovation ecosystems.

10.
CREATING VALUE FROM AN ECOSYSTEM

Innovation ecosystems need to create a value chain that meets the aims of all the entities involved. Everyone involved in ecosystem development needs to strike a balance between the immediate and real priorities of their own organisation and the wider and perhaps more diffuse priorities of the system itself. These may not always appear to be directly aligned; however, these systems are only successful when there is a value chain that meets the aims of all organisations involved and this value can be realised by concerted action among all the agents. All entities must therefore be able to recognise this value and be prepared to act in concert.

Let's use a real example from the innovation ecosystem for sports footwear (Paine 2014). In the early 2000s, an organisation called DyeCoo patented the world's first waterless dying technology, with the potential to significantly reduce the impact on the environment and reduce processing costs. Large, branded apparel businesses within the ecosystem, such as Nike and Adidas, had several strategies that they could play in relation to this new technology. Traditionally, large companies such as Nike might have pursued exclusive ownership over the intellectual property (IP). However, in today's world of commercial R&D, processes are more complex, and companies such as Nike have also factored in the world's depleting resources as one of the major threats to its commercial success. Sole ownership of this IP would not bring them a competitive advantage in the long term, even if they could secure it. It was no longer in their overall best interests to own this innovation, but they needed to find ways to leverage it in a manner that built commercial, reputational advantage while deepening their knowledge base in the short and long term. The answer for Nike and DyeCoo was to build a partnership enabling Nike to play a leadership role revolutionising the textile industry while leveraging external R&D expertise.

Today, innovation is increasingly dependent on flexibility and agility. Companies must be able to switch in and out of using in-house capabilities, open-source systems, commissioned activities, outsourced services, and key partnerships to respond to the dynamics of business and markets.

The different elements and assets within these ecosystems need to be connected by both human and digital means into a network that delivers. In innovation ecosystems, the way these individual entities relate to each other and the position they occupy are important. Iansiti and Levien (2004) described three broad business ecosystem strategies that a firm typically adopts:

- *Keystone* – concerned with the overall health of the ecosystem, enhancing connections and durability, and deeply invested in its survival.
- *Dominator* – concerned primarily with monopolising an ecosystem and/or constant value extraction.
- *Niche player* – operating specialised capabilities and typically responsible for most of the value creation within a network.

Keystone organisations will often have the most to gain (and the most to lose) from an ecosystem, but can also assert the most influence on value chains and knowledge flows. In many innovation ecosystems, these organisations aim to nurture and improve the overall health of the ecosystem. However, all ecosystem participants must be able to benefit from and influence the network for the ecosystem to be effective.

One way to do this is to try and simplify how network participants interact, enabling an environment in which all parts
of the network can be agile, responsive, and collaborative. For
these reasons, long-term relationships are a useful means to
create a stable environment and facilitate the exchange of value
created within the system. Figure 2 shows how a company can
sit at a key position within an innovation ecosystem, and it
describes the web of interdependent relationships that have
formed. This is based on a real case study, though the company
and partner identifiers have been removed.

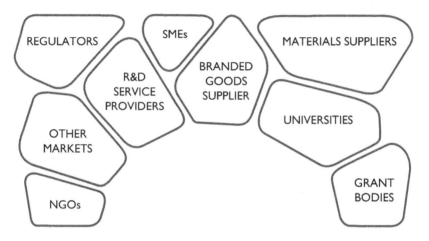

*Figure 2: Examples of positioning in an innovation ecosystem
network.*

Capturing value for your organisation from its work in an
innovation ecosystem is a function of (1) the set of organisations in the network, (2) your own position in that network
of relationships, and (3) the type of *control position* your
company can assert over particular assets (patents, trade
secrets, computer programs, databases, assay protocols,

physical innovation spaces, and equipment, etc.). For example, in some sectors, such as pharma and bioscience, a patent remains a fundamentally important legal means to claim control over an invention. A granted patent is a governmental recognition that for a limited time, the patented technology is the property of a company — which can then be transacted or used to raise capital.

In addition to your positioning within an ecosystem, you must also consider the control position you will be able to create on key assets — for example, whether you own something, or can exert significant influence, or whether your company has a weaker control position. Increasingly, even your proprietary innovations will make use of some of the same elements and assets that are available to your competitors.

In Table 4 we give a non-exhaustive list of asset control positions that a company can use in protecting and exploiting an innovation. We've identified six key asset control positions, and the type of influence that is associated with those positions. These range from an asset that is owned by your company, where you have full control over its use, through to assets that are in the public domain, where you have no control position, though there are also no restrictions on use. As a company moves from a 'closed by default' mindset towards a more open innovation approach, R&D leaders begin to switch their thinking from 'what is the minimum I can get away with sharing?' to 'what do I really need to avoid sharing?' In this shift, the control positions described here provide a rich set of opportunities.

These control positions are also available to the other actors in the innovation ecosystem. They will have assets that they own but can make available to you to create value. By keeping this in mind, the partnerships you can form will give you an opportunity to create more value than a closed approach would generate, and through this you can benefit from innovation assets that you do not own.

ASSET TYPE	DESCRIPTION
Owned	The asset is 100% legally owned and controlled by the company. Examples include physical assets such as land, buildings, and equipment, but also intangible assets such as granted patents or copyrights.
Hard Control	The asset is NOT legally owned by the company, but the company has secured some legally binding control over aspects of how it can be used.
Soft Control	The company has no formal or legal control of the asset, but it has created another effective means to influence and direct how the asset is best used. Trade secrets are often examples of a soft-control position.
Open	The company can freely use and/or remix and/or share improvements in an asset, but has no means to further control the asset. Changes made to open assets will often need to be completed on the same terms that the original asset was made available.
Public Domain	No restrictions on use, but no control position.
API	An application programming interface (API) is a digital connection to the output of an algorithm working on a dataset. A company can use an API to benefit from digital innovation capabilities offered by another organisation. It can also use an API, under terms of a licence, to control access to the company's digital assets with an exquisite level of fine control that is not possible using licences on patented technologies.

Table 4: Asset control positions that exist within innovation ecosystems.

Increasingly, the role of senior R&D leaders will be to design, build, and nurture innovation ecosystems, curating the different elements and assets and how they all connect. This creates new challenges, such as being able to understand which elements of an ecosystem can be controlled or influenced as part of the whole network and to maintain the connections between different elements and assets. You will need to be able to shift the focus of your work from delivering agreed outcomes to supporting emergent outcomes, be able to generate and measure value from emergent work, and be confident in maintaining a wider range of control positions. Appraising exactly how much of your work needs to be kept confidential or fully owned by your company is core to working in an innovation ecosystem.

The following steps provide a simple way for you to start to understand the potential of your existing networks to become effective innovation ecosystems.

- Write down your full vision/ambition, with a deliberate disregard for the resources that are in your direct control (staff members, external budgets, lab facilities).
- Assume, for the time being, that partners outside your company can be found to fill in the gaps required to achieve your full ambition.
- Capture the role that your company and its partners are playing in a network or ecosystem that you are involved in. Things to consider are (1) place (keystone, dominator, or niche), (2) goal (what each of them wants from the ecosystem), (3) assets and control positions, and (4) key connections.
- Loosely sketch out the network or ecosystem.
- Add in the connections or interactivity between the organisations on this particular programme.
- Label the connectors if there is something special about the connection (e.g., Strategic Partnership, Non-Exclusive Licence, Joint Development Agreement, or key common staff).

II.
COMPARING
ORGANISATIONS

There are significant differences in the organisational constraints universities operate under, when compared to commercial R&D, that enable them to build specialised knowledge bases. For example, they typically have a higher degree of flexibility in the overall size and shape of their staff base. Although university staff typically work within the context of year-long workplans, and are reasonably inflexible within these workplans, universities as institutions can reshape their staffing much more flexibly than most companies, recruiting specialised and skilled talent into two- or three-year fixed-term postdoctoral contracts. They rarely try to retrain existing specialist staff. The expectation in most research-intensive universities is that specialised staff will, at the end of their contract period, either continue to another temporary post at the same university or move to another university or to a company. Unless the institution is looking to develop a strategic capability in a specific area, it is unlikely that staff will secure a more permanent position on the salaried faculty. A simple comparison is shown below.

COMMERCIAL	ORGANISATIONAL CAPABILITY	UNIVERSITY
Low	Short-term staffing flexibility	High
High	Procurement flexibility	Low
Medium to high	Agility (fast change of focus)	Low
Low	Multi-year budgeting	High
Medium to low	Knowledge-base resilience	High
Low	Capital expenditure (CAPEX) budget flexibility	High
Medium	Leverage potential	High

Table 5: Comparison of corporate and university organisations.

12.
WHY UNIVERSITIES PARTNER WITH COMPANIES

Universities are drawn to the scale of large businesses, their corporate reputations, the products they develop, and the problems they are seeking to address. For the corporate side of the university, large company brands are a strong pull. Universities will use the corporate brand to attract students – often as evidence of the type of educational experiences they will receive and to illustrate their potential prospects after graduation. Additionally, corporate badging demonstrates the relevance of academic research to society.

Below the waterline, there are a wide range of intrinsic and extrinsic motivations driving researchers to partner with commercial organisations. Primarily, you will find that researchers are interested in the unique challenges and problems that a commercial organisation can pose. These challenges will require some translation into academically viable research questions, but the interest they will have in prototyping alongside a company's access to markets, and ultimately consumers, means that a company can often create opportunities for researchers to develop and apply fundamental knowledge to 'real-world' problems. You will also find that researchers are being increasingly driven to contribute to the knowledge economy and are now expected to be able to demonstrate impact from their activities. Universities are also drawn to working with small and medium-sized businesses (SMEs). Here the barriers to engagement are different, but the benefits to a university are equally attractive. These include a much more direct impact of innovation projects on the overall business performance of an SME, a chance for employment of recent graduates, and the rooting that SMEs have in different social and economic networks compared to larger companies.

In the UK, for example, the funding body responsible for research and innovation defines impact in relation to the contribution to society and the economy:

> Impact is the 'demonstrable contribution that excellent research makes to society and the economy'. This occurs in many ways – through creating and sharing new knowledge and innovation; inventing ground-breaking new products, companies and jobs; developing new and improving existing public services and policy; enhancing quality of life and health; and many more.
>
> (UKRI 2019)

There are two key fields of impact that are worth keeping in mind when having discussions with academics and university leaders. *Academic impact* is the type of contribution that the university's excellent research is making to advancing scientific knowledge, across and within disciplines, including significant advances in understanding, method, theory, and application. This type of impact is quantified through analysis of publications from key researchers within the university, peer review, etc. *Economic and societal impact* is the contribution that the university's research excellence has made to wider society, and in many cases also to the wider economy.

In the Netherlands, for example, research impact is assessed through what is known as the Standard Evaluation Protocol (VSNU 2014). In keeping with other OECD countries, the assessment criteria in this activity focus on (1) research quality, i.e. the contribution to the field of knowledge, (2) relevance to society, i.e. quality, scale, and relevance of specific economic, social, or cultural target groups, and (3) viability, i.e. the resources and capabilities of the research unit including facilities, governance, and research leadership.

In short, impact can be defined as *evidence of both invention and innovation*. Many universities in the twenty-first century are increasingly regarding themselves not just as the generator of great ideas, but also as a primary source of knowledge and competence that can play a more direct and positive role in the economic, social, and cultural life of the cities, regions, and countries in which they operate. These impacts are not created through the publication of scientific papers, but through consulting work, provision of high-quality technical services, undertaking competitive and pre-competitive contract research and discovery, and by acting as hosts and partners in co-created open-access infrastructure.

Throughout your interactions with researchers at a particular university, you will find that each individual will place a different emphasis on the importance they personally see in creating economic and societal impact from their work. However, very few academic scientists remain solely focused on pure research and the search for fundamental knowledge without some concern for application. Many are more orientated towards solving problems that are posed in the 'real world', and while they are still interested in fundamental knowledge, the questions that they are addressing are inspired by the users of research. You will also find researchers who are mostly interested in applied research, where choices and action are predominantly driven by the goal of problem solution.

For most companies, the real strength of a research-intensive university is its ability to discover novel algorithms, materials, processes, and insights. Often this work will be some distance from commercial or societal application. Innovate UK's Technology Readiness Level (TRL) framework is a useful way to understand where opportunities for collaborations are concentrated (NASA 1974). Much, though certainly not all, university research activity will be concentrated towards TRL levels 1–3, although there are many higher education institutions and research institutes that would position their interests and activities at higher levels of technology readiness.

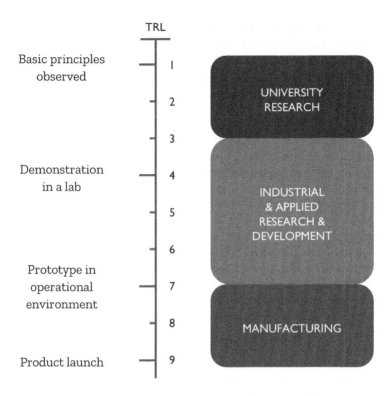

TRL

Basic principles observed — 1

2

3

Demonstration in a lab — 4

5

6

Prototype in operational environment — 7

8

Product launch — 9

UNIVERSITY RESEARCH

INDUSTRIAL & APPLIED RESEARCH & DEVELOPMENT

MANUFACTURING

Figure 3: University research and its technology readiness level (TRL).

Disciplinary differences may influence where on this framework university research is located. If you are working with a biologist, physicist, or mathematician, it is quite likely that their work will be some distance from commercial or societal application. In the health sciences, social sciences, and engineering there is an increased propensity towards applied or user-inspired research. Ultimately, university research occupies an earlier TRL compared with corporate research, and this can be a key driver of the differences in intrinsic and extrinsic alignment between the aims of commercial research and academic research.

COMMERCIAL RESEARCHER		UNIVERSITY RESEARCHER
Creation of new-to-the-world knowledge	=	Creation of new-to-the-world knowledge
Primarily driven by business need	≠	Primarily driven by academic curiosity
Seeks the highest commercial impact	≠	Seeks the widest possible publication
Coherent with corporate strategic direction	≠	Coherent with the career direction of the individual

Table 6: Intrinsic alignment between commercial and university researchers.

13.
SETTING EXPECTATIONS

Based on our experience of working with universities, there are three things that companies should not *generally expect* to get from a university as an institution.

- Do not expect routine early access to a stream of newly created technology-based spin-outs or commercially lucrative licence deals arising from the university's core academic research. Some universities will spin out companies as a matter of course, and some have been very successful at this. However, both their ability to do this and their level of motivation will be based on their specific context (which includes their founding remit and the relative importance of public and private funding into the university). Note that once a spin-out has been created, it will inevitably diverge in style, governance, and focus from the university research team that it came from. Engaging with university spin-outs and other start-up companies is not in scope for this playbook.
- Don't ask them to work in ways that really do not play to their strengths. Knowing what your partners are actually good at is key to building a partnership. Try to identify what exactly the university team is great at – it is this that you should cherish and leverage. In some cases, you might find that how the academics drive their research programmes may be more valuable to you than the content of their programmes.

Very few academic researchers are better at commercialising technology than you are, or other partners of yours are, so it is best not to expect them to do that.

- Don't try to get them to align their research direction to yours. They will only do this if there is an intrinsic desire to do so.

Universities are large complex institutions with a wealth of knowledge and resources that can be difficult to access. It can take time to orientate yourself and to understand what motivates the individuals and the organisation as a whole. A general understanding of what universities are typically good at and interested in can help you to understand what you are looking for in a partnership. Undertaking some rapid research into the specific institution you are working with, or considering partnering with, can assist and help direct you to where you need to go.

14.
MAPPING INTERACTIONS

This section presents a framework to help you map the different tactical and operational interactions that can take place in a company–university engagement. It will help you determine how best to define different project types and relationships between your company and a university partner.

Identifying who to work with within a university can take a considerable investment of time in the first instance. There is rarely a one-stop shop for contacting academics within universities, and even where there is a centralised department helping facilitate relationships with external companies, you will still need to have a clear idea of what is available, and why you want to partner. Our experience is that university professional services staff, often in Tech Transfer Offices (TTO) and business gateways, aspire to being a one-stop shop for external access to the university. However, the complexity of department, school, and faculty structures, the limited scale of TTO resources, and the fact that TTO staff work at some distance from the detail and scope of the university's knowledge assets, mean that it is often only possible for TTOs to signpost and facilitate. Although this is in and of itself valuable, it falls short of a one-stop shop. For that reason, we would encourage readers not to stop there. A relationship manager will need to include the TTO and other university professional staff in their list of active contacts, but this should not stop them reaching beyond the TTO, nor should they expect the TTO to do this work for them.

As a first step, we encourage you to look at what is published in corporate promotional materials (such as annual reviews, strategy reports, and the university website) to find out what they are already doing, the academic leaders who work there, what capabilities they have, and the potential services they could provide. For example, do they have a microscopy imaging suite or a psychology lab? What are their research specialisms?

Consideration of a university's resources and expertise will generate a list of areas that you may be interested in. However, by itself this is not very helpful for framing what you might do together. So, to help with this, we developed the interactions quadrant to capture the different types of interaction that can be established between your company and a university partner.

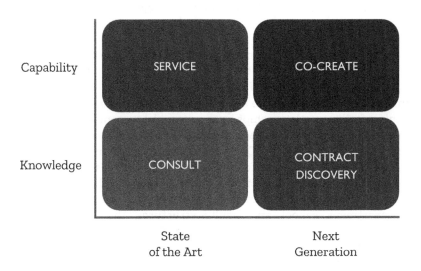

Figure 4: The company–university interactions quadrant.

Specific company–university interactions are spread out across two axes. The horizontal axis is the level of stretch required in the piece of work you are looking to do. The vertical axis is the type of asset that you are trying to access in the university.

We assume that a good-quality university department is already research active, working at state of the art, and keen to create the next generation. The department will have two distinct sets of academic assets. First, they will have a body of knowledge about a field of science and technology and, second, they will have a set of capabilities that they use to drive their field of research (for example, laboratories, equipment, assays, software platforms, tricks of the trade and experimental techniques).

This quadrant framework arose from our experience. We found that it was unhelpful and confusing to treat all university projects as if they were the same. Creating clarity between your company needs and the capabilities and staff that a university has to offer is the first step to a successful project. The quadrant results in four categories of interaction:

- *Service*. Access to pre-existing capabilities such as data processing, specialised measurement equipment, or fully serviced and equipped lab space.
- *Consulting*. Academic experts acting as advisors using their existing knowledge and understanding of their specialist field.
- *Contract discovery*. Commissioning research in the university to create new knowledge, the results of which you will own as intellectual property (IP).
- *Co-creating*. The discovery of new knowledge based capabilities in partnership, often part funded by your company and part funded by government grants, with some form of pre-agreed IP exploitation arrangement.

A particular company–university partnership will be very specific to the ambition of the university; the specific science area and company lead; and details of the local funding, tax, and legal regimes. However, we have found that in any collaboration the portfolio of individual activities that are driven in partnership will be close to the four distinct types above.

There are many different ways in which you can use this tool. You can start to map out how you might want to work with a university in the first instance, as is demonstrated in the completed example in Figure 5. It is a way of structuring your initial desk research process and will help you get below the tip of the iceberg. You can use it in conversation with your university partner, either as a populated chart to show them what you've found out and to invite them to add to it, or as a general framework to highlight the types of things that you could do together.

Quite often when we put this framework in front of university leaders and academics they will take out their smart phones and take a picture of it. They find that it is equally helpful for them as it is for us to articulate some possibilities. Quite often we will return to it throughout negotiations and ongoing collaborative work. We often turn to it while the partnership is in flight; it helps to organise and visualise what we are doing and can be used as a crucial step for the formalisation of an emerging partnership.

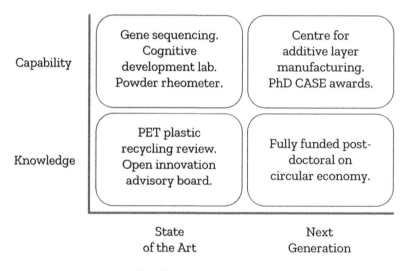

Figure 5: Completed example of the interactions quadrant.

Another way of using the framework is to help you prioritise where you might start a relationship. Universities are sometimes wary of industrial innovation projects because of their preconceptions of what a company might expect in terms of ownership of IP. Their perception is that standard commercial contracting terms will be structured so that the company will own 100% of the IP from a project. Equally, we often find that universities have unrealistic expectations of the value of patents and the time it takes to transfer a patent into a product and bring it to market. The framework can help you to differentiate between the various activities that you could do together and to find 'safe zones' in which to begin a partnership, circumventing potentially lengthy and protracted negotiations.

Each of the four zones of the quadrant carries distinct characteristics in terms of outputs, risks, costs, time to market/impact, and IP. These are described in Table 7. For example, in the service quadrant the data that is created will often be fully owned by your company, while any IP created through improving the methodology will remain in the university's control. In the contract discovery quadrant, your company is commissioning the academic institution to create new knowledge or technology and will own the output, whereas in co-creation these activities might only be partially funded and the IP arrangements may be more complex. The quadrant risk table maps these differences out in more detail.

QUADRANT	FUNDING, RISKS, AND INTELLECTUAL PROPERTY
Service	This is often competitively priced and low risk. The company owns the new data, which will have immediate utility. If any new methodology IP is created through the analysis of company samples, this IP will likely be retained by the academic partner for use in other projects.
Co-create	This work is co-funded by the company and public money. Risk is medium. The company cannot usually own the arising IP outright, so some form of agreement about how this is dealt with needs to be negotiated. These negotiations can be protracted.
Consult	Costs are negotiable and the work is low risk. New method or technology IP is not created from this type of activity. Company owns all specialist advice. Often an academic will be inspired after these interactions to create new research routes and ideas.
Contract Discovery	The cost of these projects is high, and fully funded by the company. They are, by definition, medium–high risk. However, the output can be of high strategic value, and IP is normally 100% controlled by the company. Contract negotiations can be protracted, and will focus on IP ownership, publications, milestones, and outcomes.

Table 7: Interactions quadrant: funding, risk, and IP.

For a university department that is new to working in partnership with your company, it may be best to begin with a series of consulting or service interactions. These activities are relatively low cost and low risk and should not create protracted negotiations. If these types of activity are unsuccessful (or the negotiations are very protracted and convoluted), it is a good indication that a deeper and more strategic partnership is unlikely or impossible. Conversely, successful consulting and service activities are often very useful foundations on which to build more strategic co-creation activities.

The opportunity to participate in projects of any type with a university will be bounded by the resources and assets available. Large companies, with well-known brands, can sustain the attention of universities for long periods of time before a project begins. Smaller companies may, at first, feel that they cannot compete with these behemoths; however, once a project has started, all projects run through the same management system in the university. It is the difference between talking at the tip of the iceberg and working to create valuable new knowledge below the waterline. We do not recommend smaller businesses, without a well-known public face, to start at the top, but rather, do the research to find the specific academics who will have the skills to help you. In Section 17 (Defining the Problem), we will give you some tools to help you to define your business needs in a way that will engage academic scientists – and they always respond to interesting problems.

Universities recognise that smaller companies have relevant capabilities that are difficult to find elsewhere. They value the flexibility and deep commitment that small and medium-sized enterprises (SMEs) bring to projects. The exposure to all the different facets of running a business gives SMEs an edge when universities want to create spin-out businesses. Often SMEs are strongly rooted in a specific community (geographic, social, or topical) and their inclusion in projects allows the university to demonstrate direct impact in these communities.

A good way to structure a co-creation project is to define two elements: (1) a new methodology – where the arising IP is owned by the university and details of the method will be widely published, and (2) application of this new method to the company problem, which will create insights that are private to the company.

We recognise smaller businesses are unlikely to start university relationships with a contract discovery project in the way that a larger company may do, and the daily fee rates for consulting may seem prohibitive. But there are many opportunities to use university services and jointly seek grant funding for small co-creation projects. Some flexibility over IP is all that is needed – you don't need to own the patent (with the inherent costs and risks), you just need access on the best possible terms.

Finally, it is important to recognise that the contractual negotiations required within each quadrant will vary signifi-cantly. The creation of mutually acceptable contractual terms for contract discovery activities is necessarily high cost and can be very involved in terms of the complexity of the IP negotiation process.

You should set aside dedicated time and resources to establish these types of projects unless there is a pre-existing agreement, in which case much of the negotiations can be bypassed. In the UK for example, the full economic cost payable by a company for a postdoctoral position can often be in excess of €125K per person per annum. Sometimes a grant may be available to augment the investment a company would make, but this cost will need to be covered one way or another. Due to the complexity of the IP negotiations, companies who are undertaking this type of project are advised to budget for a considerable amount of effort, over a considerable lapsed timescale, to set these projects up.

15.
BUILDING A STRATEGIC APPROACH TO PARTNERSHIP

In this section, we set out some of the benefits of creating a more strategic approach in your company to university partnerships, and provide a set of tools to identify areas of alignment in existing or potential university partners.

Over the past decade there has been a marked increase in the number of research relationships between companies and universities. The term *partnership* is, however, frequently misappropriated to describe straightforward business relationships. It is not possible for an organisation to have more than a handful of strategic partnerships because of the time and resources that are needed to maintain them. Alternative forms of company–university partnership that may be a better label for your current collaborations include:

- *Bilateral project.* An ad hoc or one-off project that may involve external funding and shared goals. Risks in this type of project need to be encapsulated in the legal agreement that is put in place (mitigation measures). It is a transactional engagement with no particular expectation of ongoing activity.
- *Joint Development Agreement.* A sustained activity, or connected set of discrete activities, where two

organisations work together on a large shared-risk project. This might include the pursuit of funding and/or the development of resources.

- *Innovation Umbrella Agreement.* A formal or informal agreement between individuals or organisations to achieve a common goal. Similar to a strategic partnership, the arrangements can develop goodwill and lead to multiple projects. However, they are typically less focused on the creation of new knowledge, and may have a shorter term. They are more typical for company–company innovation partnerships than company–university relationships.

Strategic partnerships are underpinned by a high-level arrangement across an entire department, cluster of departments, or businesses. This arrangement will pull together a portfolio of projects, resources, and capabilities under a shared framework that enables greater cooperation and innovation across two or more organisations. To be effective, a strategic partnership must be aligned with the vision, values, and objectives of both organisations over a sustained period, usually no less than three to five years. From experience, we have found that in developing strategic partnerships, we open the possibilities of co-investment in strategic capabilities and for co-branding opportunities, which can be used to access funding and achieve greater impact.

A good partnership can accelerate the beneficial blending of the two research cultures of universities and industry: the discovery-driven culture of the university and the commercial-driven culture of the company. This also helps to build social capital and foster a culture of openness and transparency across the two organisations. This is a transition from contract-led interactions to human-led relationships, enabling conversations and plans based on knowledge of one another's strengths and gaps. In summary, several benefits emerge from strategic partnerships:

- More flexible patenting and intellectual property (IP) arrangements.
- Greater understanding of each other's priorities, pressures, and ways of working.
- Finding common ground on confidentiality and non-disclosure arrangements.
- The creation of reciprocal arrangements (for example, companies can benefit from some of the best graduates).
- Seeding and influencing the direction of early-stage research (for example, through funding PhD studentships).
- Rapid access to cutting-edge scientific expertise and immediate application to business challenges.
- Creating deep research strengths in your focus areas.
- Obtaining higher levels of leveraged funding.

A strategic partnership will not come out of the blue. If you have had limited prior experience working with a partner, you would not start the relationship by forming a strategic partnership. They are often built on years of partnering and high levels of trust across two organisations.

16.
A STRATEGIC PARTNERSHIP MODEL

This section describes six levels on which a partnership should be built and evaluated. Whether your partnership is embryonic or well established, whether you are negotiating a cooperative agreement or simply assessing who to work with, it is important to reflect on the different layers of a partnership.

The vision and mission of most partnerships will often remain quite stable over a long period. They are an articulation of why and how the partners are working together – essentially the change they want to see in the world. In the case of partnering with universities there is often a strong alignment with the company's vision so that both partners can pursue their passion for science that matters, and a shared desire for the new ideas (and ultimately new products and services) to make a difference in the world.

At the mission level, you might typically look for ways in which partnering can be beneficial to helping your organisation achieve its goals while recognising the needs of a partner to accomplish theirs. For example, corporates are increasingly turning to universities because of their mission to generate new foundational knowledge. This gives the company access to their capabilities in early-stage research as opposed to funding this in-house. Conversely, universities are increasingly turning to organisations such as corporates to exploit their mission to launch products. This gives them access to substantial product development capabilities that they can use as a conduit for showing effective industrial engagement and research impact.

The strategic level of the partnership needs to demonstrate a real shared plan, including aspects of governance, funding, risk sharing, arising intellectual assets, and communications. The operational plan needs to deal with some of the mechanics required to achieve the plan: regular liaison, resolving issues, unblocking barriers.

For innovation partnerships in general, and for partnerships with academic institutions, tactical activities are also crucial. Often a project will be tactical – it will be aligned to the strategic plan, but will not in and of itself achieve the strategic goal. Tactical work also requires an opportunistic exploitation of changes in the environment. For example, there may be a broad agreement and understanding in the partnership that the strategic plan requires a multi-million euro investment in a new shared capability. Unless and until a specific funding opportunity arises, this strategic intent is unlikely to become a reality. This type of funding opportunity may arise from specific operational work, e.g., influencing at government level, but more often these opportunities will arise from unexpected externalities or events, or chance encounters. A great strategic partnership is able to mobilise itself rapidly behind a tactical opportunity because the strategic relevance is immediately obvious to both or all of the partners.

The levels framework can be used at an early stage in forming a partnership to co-create what the partnership will be about and how the partners will work together on each of the levels.

LEVEL	DESCRIPTION
Vision	Why we want to change the world.
Mission	How we are going to change the world.
Objectives	The specific things we want to happen.
Strategy	The long-term plan (including all likely environmental changes) to achieve objectives.
Operational	The ongoing, slow-changing, day-to-day machinery to achieve the strategy.
Tactical	The elements of the plan that flex as opportunities arise or the environment changes.

Table 8: Framework for building alignment in strategic partnerships.

Taking a hypothetical example, a company might have the *vision* to reverse the negative impacts of plastic on the environment and drive cleaner economic growth. A *mission* arising from this stance could establish a partnership of world-leading innovators in sustainable plastics, delivering cleaner growth and reducing plastic waste. *Objectives* are then set to create innovations that deliver 100% of plastic packaging to be reusable, recyclable, or compostable, while also eliminating single-use packaging. The *strategy* to achieve these objects might be to create a circular economy in plastic packaging, addressing the biggest and most visible issues, and then to create solutions that can be used across other plastic value chains. *Operationally*, a joint executive team would lead and deliver on this long-term plan with a broader advisory group ensuring progress is measured. This then frees the executive team to flex their resources, delivery mechanisms, and approaches to exploit *tactical* opportunities as the external landscape evolves.

The ambition behind strategic partnerships is to set up a means for your company to address its biggest problems. When building a strategic partnership with a university it is worth keeping the following six aims in mind:

- Promote your company as a partner of choice for universities.
- Maximise opportunities to work with other strategic partners.
- Explore opportunities for cross-partnership working.
- Leverage government funding and other funding sources.
- Ensure that your work with strategic partners is quicker and easier for your researchers compared with other universities.
- Translate your problems into meaningful science problems worth solving.

There are many strategies you can use to identify and choose where and who to partner with; however, as a rule of thumb, we have used the following criteria:

- They have a mutual interest in game-changing ideas and innovation.
- They have knowledge and/or capability that you want access to.
- They see you as strategically important to fulfilling their aims and objectives over the long term.
- They are accessible from one of your company locations.
- There is an ability to grow the relationship over time and across your business and their institution.
- They have an interest in developing the nature of the work they do with you.
- They understand the commercial environment, and the differences in its culture and drivers.

There are clear benefits of an appropriately aligned strategic partnership, from access to capabilities and opportunities for leveraging external funding through to reduced transaction costs and increased social capital. For these reasons, the end of a strategic partnership is always business critical. This is because they have given you access to a large range of capabilities and resources that you would not be able to access otherwise. One simple way to ascertain whether a partnership with a university is strategic or not is to reflect on how much it would matter if the partnership were to end.

Below is a set of simple, staged questions and exercises to bootstrap your thinking on strategic partnerships.

- Articulate a vision, mission, and set of objectives for a proposed or existing strategic academic partnership.
- How well can you articulate the benefits of this to your company colleagues?
- How well does your academic partner understand the articulation?
- Now ask your opposite number in the academic partner to do the same. How do the two descriptions and ambitions compare?
- Consider how you can create light-touch but effective means to govern and guide a partnership as it formulates and executes strategy and operations.
- Map out the strategic, operational, and tactical activities that are required for different elements of your partnership – for example, corporate-level activity, research projects, building capabilities, studentships, and joint communications.
- How can you ensure that there are successful tactical projects created and executed?
- Who in your company needs to meet with whom in the university to keep operational work going? And how often?
- What funding or other resources are available to you to support the building of a relationship?

17.
DEFINING THE PROBLEM

This section will help you to articulate a technical problem that your company wants to address in a language that enables your potential academic partners to see where they could contribute their expertise.

Leveraging resources and knowledge from a university requires that you must first be able to effectively define the problem that you want to work on and articulate what you already know and are doing in this area. This is equally the case whether the science is new and emerging or whether it is a mature capability.

It is important to university partners that a company brings their biggest problems and those that need big solutions from the brain trusts that are available in academia. While the technical challenges that your business faces have the potential to be interesting and worth solving for researchers, there is still work needed to set the brief at the right level and to define the scientific problem to make it an attractive proposition. Articulating the 'science problem' at the right degree of granularity and translating your company 'R&D speak' and 'business speak' into language that resonates well with academics is a key part of setting up a relationship.

This is not something to be done in isolation. In Section 27 (Working in Partnership) we suggest some tools for working with universities and other potential collaborators such as industry and government. It is important not to underestimate the importance of getting this right. University partners often report that they are more motivated by interesting science than by revenue generated through the partnerships. Furthermore, while impact (through publication) of the research is a clear and obvious driver, so is the knowledge that their work can be applied through a route to market that they do not otherwise have access to.

In commercial R&D, the science problem tends to be articulated in terms of what is required by the business. This is often not interesting to academic partners, who are typically triggered by the search for fundamental knowledge either through basic research or through investigating real-world problems. For a question to be interesting for a university researcher there must be a hypothesis that needs to be proven or disproven.

The following is a well-known adage about sharing (Brannan 1949): 'If you and I have an apple each and we exchange them, then we will still have one apple each. But if you and I both have ideas and we exchange them, then each of us will have two ideas'. If the ideas that are being exchanged are non-trivial, then idea exchange will also involve translation.

Translation always requires the expenditure of *interpretive labour* (Graeber 2015). This is creative and often difficult work. Interpretive labour is equal to the energy put into explaining an idea, plus the energy needed to understand it. Although in principle it doesn't matter in this equation whether the explanation or understanding requires the larger energy expenditure, in practice this situation is never symmetrical. When a commercial innovator is working with a university, it is always the case that a good translation, the shift from commercial requirement into common scientific discourse, requires more energy from the company than from the academic. While there are people working in universities who can help with this translation (i.e. knowledge transfer departments) – and you will find that some researchers are very adept at doing this with you – frequently this translation load will fall onto your company R&D teams.

If the requisite amount of interpretive labour is not invested by the company, then translation from a company problem to an academically rich and interesting set of problems is unlikely to be successful. To help with this type of translation, we have developed a 'Science WANT' template. We have used this in several different ways. For example, before meeting with a researcher we might complete the template to help organise our thinking and frame the conversation. Once developed, we may share it with a technology transfer department in the university who can use it to articulate a problem in a way that is interesting to their researchers and also connect us to the people who might be keen to work with us. We have also used a full set of completed templates as a framework for conversations in a workshop. We find it tends to help us surface a network of expertise that can be brought to bear on a particular challenge. It is rare that we find an exact match to the problem that we are looking to solve, but it is also rare not to find something really useful.

THE PROBLEM	DESCRIPTION
Description	A short description of the core scientific challenge to be tackled.
What do you know already?	Pertinent background know-how. Suitable for non-commercial scientists to understand your scientific depth and breadth in the challenge area. Do not assume that what you take for common knowledge is also common in the academic team.
What don't you know already?	The specific areas of the problem where you know you have a poorer level of understanding. Explain, if possible, why there is a poorer level of understanding.
What data do you have on the problem?	The data you already have at your disposal. This will help academic scientists to gauge the degree of your quantitative understanding. They may suggest analysis and enquiry routes. They may immediately identify pertinent data available from other sources.
Scientific phenomena and hypotheses	These could be based on experiences, guesses, intuition, hunches, published papers, or anomalous/unexplained phenomena.
Measurement techniques you already use	These may include generic techniques as applied to the problem, specific company test methods, or industry standards. Make sure you include your understanding of the accuracy and precision you can achieve with these techniques.

Table 9: Science WANT template.

Working through the prompts in this template helps your research partners to see what it is you are doing and to articulate your problems in a way that is scientifically relevant. In using this framework, you will give your partners a grasp of potential areas of mutual interest on which you can work together. It can be used to reveal existing capabilities as well as potential projects.

18.
CREATING LEVERAGE

In the next two sections, we present a framework designed to capture the impact of company R&D investments in the specific projects and activities of strategic partnerships. This section provides guidance on how to use the methodology in a transparent way.

Over the past ten years we have been able to develop a simple but useful way to quantify the benefits of the social capital a company has built with academic partners. This approach is encapsulated in the concept of *leverage*. With this concept in mind, it is possible to develop approaches that help your company to utilise the resources of other organisations to maximise advantage, while maintaining and enriching partnerships. This leverage methodology will allow you to quantify why you have been successful and the degree of that success.

These resources can come directly from a university partner, but more often will come from organisations outside the formal partnership between your company and the university. These organisations might typically include the science and innovation funding agencies of central or regional government organisations, or key grant-awarding non-government organisations (NGOs), such as the Bill and Melinda Gates Foundation. Sometimes there are also opportunities to leverage resources from other private companies that have common, non-competing, scientific interests. Leveraging external R&D funding can help a company to:

- Increase the speed, efficiency, and agility of your innovation activities.
- Support longer investment horizon projects than you are normally able to support.
- Access science capabilities through partnering that act as a multiplier to your company resources by attracting government and third-party cash.
- Access capabilities that would be impossible with your R&D external budgets alone.

A strategic and structured approach to accessing external innovation funds and assets requires a clear understanding of how to maximise the benefits from external grants, R&D infrastructure and subsidies, through partnership rather than via direct funding into the company. Helping partners to secure R&D funding to deliver company outcomes is very often better than receiving money directly. This approach helps to avoid the requirements of specific state-aid audits, exposure to changes in government priorities during the funded project period, and external administration requirements. It can also help to lower any adverse publicity that can sometimes be associated with direct government funding to corporations. Finally, taking this approach to leverage enables a company to maintain its position as a keystone within a particular innovation ecosystem.

Company innovators will rarely have as good an understanding as a University does of the sources of government research funding that are available. Typically, a national government will take a strategic decision about the total state investment in R&D and will devolve decision making about the exact programmes and projects to funding bodies with domain expertise in innovation, engineering, physics, medicine, biology, chemistry, etc. In each of these bodies, there will be formal and informal influence networks that decide the direction of large-scale funding, and finer-grained smaller investment decisions. Typically, these lower-level decisions are made with specific 'peer-review' inputs from researchers active in the field. Governments have moved over recent years towards investments in 'grand challenges'. Often these will be defined at a macro societal impact level. Examples include, 'increased productivity', 'clean growth', and 'reducing health inequality'. Very often, the grand challenge approach will provide explicit opportunities for companies to both influence the strategic direction of programmes and also take part in research consortia. In our experience, a joint approach by a key academic thought leader and an appropriate commercial innovator to government funding bodies can be a very effective way to create a long-term leverage opportunity.

The frameworks and formula that follow in this section are here to help you quantify the value of leveraged innovation and R&D work in a way that makes sense to senior leaders, accountants, and lawyers.

There are a range of approaches, all of which would allow a company to access R&D investments that are potentially aligned with company needs and incremental to in-house R&D investments. These include:

- *Infrastructure.* Substantial innovation assets and facilities built by others, in which a company is a stakeholder and has advantage. These are very often significant infrastructure investments made by governmental or intergovernmental organisations. A company can derive a direct benefit from these assets if it can exploit a stakeholder position to align the innovation direction and activities with a company's R&D requirements.
- *Indirect grants.* Public sector, charitable, and NGO-sourced grants that other parties receive directly to fund work on company-aligned projects and programmes. Governments often allocate funding to universities and other bodies in this way for further distribution to increase the reach of funding initiatives.

- *Direct grants.* Collaborative R&D grants and subsidies for R&D activities that a company accesses to fund work on company projects and programmes. Collaborative R&D projects involving organisations from both public and private sectors is a proven driver of innovation and forms the foundation of industrial R&D investment by both individual governments, European frameworks (e.g. Horizon 2020), and internationally available funding such as the Gates Foundation.

In many countries, it is now possible for large companies that are not generally in need of government financial support to participate in collaborative R&D projects. They are often technology end-users, without the prerequisite of having to claim grant funds and undertake the associated administrative tasks involved in grant-funded projects. These 'zero-claim' projects are particularly suitable for companies who want to create a portfolio of *options* on emerging technology offerings without committing significant resources in advance. Should the technology gain traction within the company during the project, a company can then divert a much more significant internal resource to take advantage within an already defined intellectual property (IP) and confidentiality environment. These projects may also provide a company with a platform to advantageously influence government policy, create standards, or influence infrastructure investment by local and national government.

These new approaches can bring challenges to your business practices in the control of IP, management of resources, and accounting for investment. Where a company is not the sole funder, you cannot expect to exclusively 'own' or control the resulting asset, capability, IP, or knowledge. Therefore, determining the amount of resource put into a leveraged deal and what the resulting benefit of that deal might be for your company is essential. Furthermore, taking an external grant or accessing external innovation assets and facilities only makes sense if the activity supports your company's longer-term R&D strategy.

19.
ASSESSING AND CALCULATING LEVERAGE

The simplest means to calculate the value of leveraged funds is to describe the benefit your company gets from an external research and development (R&D) grant or subsidy by the amount of money your company receives directly. However, this approach does not show the full picture.

We evaluate how useful access to an external asset base may be on two distinct axes. The first is financial, where we are trying to quantify the amount of incremental, external R&D spend that is aligned with a company's needs. The second is strategic, where we qualitatively describe the degree of alignment the external assets have with a company's R&D strategic imperatives.

Below we outline some simple definitions and equations for calculating the incremental benefit that a company's R&D obtains through accessing innovation assets such as people, facilities, and funding that are outside the company. These tools can be used to help create more actionable insights around external innovation activities and support strategic decision making. Table 10 below shows the key quantities which are needed to calculate leverage.

DEFINITION	FORMULA	DESCRIPTION
Total project size	**T**	This is the investment in the specific project, not the expected value delivery to the company from a market launch. This measure sits on the financial axis.
Company contribution	**C**	Company commitment to the project, either in cash or in-kind contributions in any currency. This is the other financial measure.
Fraction of aligned work	**F**	The fraction of the work packages in the project that are directly aligned to company priorities. This is often a 'deemed' percentage rather than a fully precise measure. The company R&D project leader needs to make this call with suitable justification. This measure quantifies the degree of alignment a project has with the company's strategic direction.
Incremental R&D benefit	**IRDB** $= (T - C) \times F$	The net benefit in any currency that the company obtains from an externally funded R&D asset or activity.
Leverage	**L** $= IRDB / C$	This dimensionless quantity is the ratio of direct company contribution to the company-aligned outcomes. It is a multiplier.

Table 10: Calculating leverage.

Both leverage and IRDB can be used to describe project value in a way that captures the financial and strategic impact, but IRDB is most representative of the overall picture. Very often there are two distinct sources of the benefit that a company obtains in this type of project. In-project benefit comes from the company-relevant work packages in the project, and pre-project benefit is the value of a pre-existing innovation capability that becomes available to the company through being in the project.

We have found that the pre-project benefit can often be as high, or higher, than in-project benefit, and both of these are often much greater than the value of cash directly received by the company as part of the project. Using this leveraged innovation approach, a company can immediately benefit from much more best-in-class innovation knowledge, access to scientific equipment, expertise, and speed of execution than could be secured with just your own R&D resources.

The calculations shown can best be brought to life with an example. Here we take a hypothetical project, Project IJssel, and demonstrate the workings. Project IJssel was initiated by a technology development project funded by the Netherlands government to create a new bio-assay-based sensor system for use in the food supply chain. The sensor is based on patented IP that had already been created by the University of Nijmegen.

There are four project partners: the University of Nijmegen; ApFod BV – a small spin-out from Nijmegen that was co-founded by the inventor of the bio-assay and holds an exclusive licence to use the technology in food applications; TNO – a Dutch government-supported research organisation; and your company's R&D organisation.

Project Ijssel will begin in January 2021 and run for three

years. It has attracted a total of €1M of Netherlands government funding, to be spent across five work packages. Your company has committed €300K of in-kind effort to the project in the form of time from your food supply chain experts and also access to three company food-production facilities in Western Europe for testing sensor prototypes.

The three other project partners will commit a total of €500K to the project. Using this project information and the equations described earlier, you can calculate the leverage and incremental benefit.

> **T** – the total funding from the government and all partners in the project.
> = €1,800,000
> **C** – the company's commitment to the project, both in-kind effort and cash.
> = €300,000
> **F** – the fraction of work packages aligned to company needs, estimated by the project leader.
> = 55%
> **IRDB** – the incremental R&D benefit accruing to the company.
> = [(T – C) × F] = [(€1,800,000 – €300,000) × 0.55] = €825,000
> **L** – the multiplier of project value to company input expenditure.
> = [IRDB / C] = [€825,000 /€300,000] = 2.75

Using this basic information and these simple equations, you can quantify the additional R&D benefit the company has obtained over and above what it could do itself. This is a direct consequence of being able to partner in this government-funded project.

Project Ijssel will create an incremental R&D benefit of €825K. Furthermore, this additional benefit has been leveraged by a company investment of €300K, meaning that each company euro invested in the project has leveraged an external investment of 2.75 euros. Note that although the Netherlands government has invested the largest amount, the company has also benefited in this project from investments by the other partners in the ecosystem. So, in addition to an IRDB of nearly a million euros, the project has created a set of working relationships and trust across an ecosystem connecting an academic group, a start-up, and technology scale-up facility with the company as a potential end-user of this new technology.

Note that although the above description has been written from the point of view of a large company in an ecosystem, the same construct can and should be exploited by smaller companies. If you have innovation assets that require additional academic support, and that have a potential upside for a large end-user, you can exploit the same approach. In this type of project, you are explicitly creating options for the academic partners and the end-user, and it is your innovation role that has been able to leverage the government funding.

Over the past ten years, many large corporates have begun to shift their focus towards this open innovation approach, which utilises strategic external partnerships to access innovation assets that it neither fully owns nor fully finances. Governments are increasingly looking for impact from R&D projects, and they like to see end-users included in R&D programmes. This provides companies with a new opportunity to co-design the innovation agenda of other parties in areas of your interest. The approach detailed in this section provides a way to quantify the benefits accrued to a company's innovation efforts, and helps you to quantify the overall benefit that your company obtains from external grants, R&D infrastructure, and subsidies through these innovation partnerships.

Below we set out an approach to help you estimate the IRDB for activities around your strategic academic partnerships. Only consider time-bound research and innovation activities, where there is or will be a legally binding access arrangement to cover the activity.

- Define the beginning and end year of the activity.
- Only include incremental benefit for which a plausible cash value can be estimated.
- Describe the sources of incremental R&D benefit for the lifetime of activity. This uses a structured questioning approach, which is trying to tease out the following possible sources of benefit. Note that very often only one or two of these factors will be applicable to a given activity:
  - Third-party direct investment (cash and in-kind) into activity.
  - Prevention of cost that would be required to access and set up equivalent capability on a like-for-like basis.
  - Removal of a time delay of the expected benefit that would be incurred if the company had to set up the capability.
  - Benefit accruing from access to other people's IP and know-how.
  - Incremental improvement in transferable skills of company R&D staff through interaction with activity.
  - Increase in reputational benefit from being associated with or leading the activity.
  - Improvement of talent recruitment and retention through association with the activity.
  - Benefit from substantive progress on challenges that are de facto beyond the financial or organisational scope of the company on its own.
  - Benefit from a sharper specialisation of in-house company staff on core company activities and using other parties who are better able to run non-core activities by improving quality, flexibility, or speed.

- Benefit from all the other projects the people in the total activity have already worked on (a benefit from diversity).
  - Benefit from employing multiple people against the project aims.
- Document the assumptions and argumentation used to make the estimation of incremental benefit for each activity.
- Allocate the total IRDB into yearly buckets.

Where appropriate and/or possible, apply depreciation considerations.

20.
EXPLOITING PROXIMITY

What is too close and too far? In this section we look at how you define 'close' when talking about university partners that may be spread across the globe. We provide guidance on how to balance the different types of proximity and mitigate issues.

Traditionally, proximity is thought about in terms of geography, the spatial distance between two locations. Even in today's technology-enabled environment, geographical proximity is still important. The advantages of having an R&D presence in industry clusters near major research universities are well known. Silicon Valley, with its proximity to Stanford and the University of California-Berkeley has long been cited as an example. Close geographical proximity easily enables informal face-to-face meetings between individuals, a shared identity with respect to the locality, and co-location. We know that short distances enable people to come together, facilitating the exchange of information and tacit knowledge, but thinking in terms of geographical proximity alone is limiting. In India and China there are thousands of kilometres between institutions and company offices, but they still find ways to make these relationships work. Boschma (2005) identified four dimensions of proximity in addition to geography:

- Cognitive (what people know).
- Organisational (how activities are organised).
- Social (how people relate).
- Institutional (how institutions relate).

Cognitive proximity allows a shared knowledge base to develop, helping partners to communicate, understand, process, and absorb new information successfully.

As a rule, you tend to search for knowledge that is in close proximity to what you already know. It is a natural by-product of trying to define what you don't know, while assimilating new knowledge as it is generated. Too much cognitive proximity will stifle innovation, leading to a monoculture of ideas and low levels of creativity, narrowing perspectives of what is possible, and closing down opportunities. The right amount of cognitive proximity is essential for knowledge transfer activities to work effectively.

Organisational proximity refers to the organisational capacity of two organisations to coordinate the exchange of complementary pieces of knowledge.

Although a degree of common knowledge is needed to enable knowledge transfer, organisational capacity is also needed to maintain facilitative mechanisms that enable the exchange of knowledge between organisations. This type of proximity refers to both intra-organisational networks and to inter-organisational relationships and legal arrangements. Organisational proximity includes a consideration of the degree of economic and financial dependence within a network or ecosystem. These dependencies need not be formal legal relationships such as companies that form part of a single holding group. For example, some industrial supply chains look very hierarchical, with a single large 'prime' manufacturer that effectively imposes a demanding set of requirements on the smaller companies in the supply chain through commercial supply contracts. These networks have a very high degree of organisational proximity. However, although this proximity helps suppliers deliver incremental innovations to the prime manufacturer, larger, more ambitious innovations are difficult to prioritise in the supplier companies.

Organisational proximity between different organisations also has an impact on intellectual property (IP). Too loose a control will entail very few formal bonds between organisations and IP arrangements that could be open to misuse. Too tight a control may lead to a lack of flexibility and constraining contractual processes. Organisations tend to adopt a loose coupling between these two extremes to control opportunism and safeguard against uncertainty while maintaining flexibility.

Social proximity refers to the socially embedded relations that exist between individuals – those based on friendship, kinship, and experience.

Trust-based relationships facilitate the exchange of tacit knowledge between individuals on the micro level. They can encourage open communication modes and enable a shift away from more calculative modes such as profit and loss. This, in turn, generates the kind of lasting and committed relationships that are needed within innovation ecosystems. Where social proximity is too high, it will create closed networks that may exclude other potential partners and new ideas. It may also exert control over how things are done, locking people down into established ways of doing things to the detriment of innovation. It is widely understood that social proximity can be used to stimulate cognitive proximity, and that one of the easiest ways to stimulate social proximity is through geographical proximity, coupled with appropriate levels of organisational proximity.

Institutional proximity refers to the widely shared 'rules of the game' and values that two or more institutions are aware of and use as a matter of course. These can include common language, shared assumptions about the basis of the legal system, and IP ownership.

Whereas both organisational and social proximity refer to smaller-scale interactions between different organisations, institutional proximity refers to the larger-scale formal and informal 'institutional' frameworks of habits, routines, practices, rules, or laws that regulate the relations between organisations. These larger-scale normative frameworks can either enable or constrain how organisations work together to innovate. Some frameworks provide a stable environment for innovation, which provides a balance within an ecosystem, reducing uncertainty and opportunism while remaining open and providing opportunities for newcomers, including new partner institutions.

Institutional proximity helps create an overarching framework within which organisational and social proximity can flourish. For example, where there are low levels of institutional alignment, the ecosystem will be more affected by the levels of trust that exist on an informal level between individuals. One example of how a low level of institutional proximity can constrain a collaboration is when two organisations that are based in different legal jurisdictions struggle to come to a common agreement on the interpretation of legal terms. The authors have first-hand experience of this situation. For example, in a number of cases, we have seen collaborations between UK- and Netherlands-based organisations fail to develop, and the root cause of this failure was a low level of institutional proximity, not other factors.

Geographical proximity refers to the physical or spatial distance between the partners. Often, for companies with multiple sites, it will not be the distance between the company head office and the university, but rather the distance between the R&D team and university partner that is important.

The other dimensions of proximity are all used to compensate where there are low levels of geographical proximity, typically through technology-enhanced processes. The need for geographical proximity has therefore lessened in recent years, but it is by no means any less important than other mechanisms. Humans still crave relatedness in work, face-to-face and personal interactions, and embedded relationships will always be valuable. For many firms the physical location of their headquarters and R&D departments continues to be a key consideration in terms of potential collaborators, access to networks, and high-quality people.

►◄

Although the formation of this tool is academic in origin, and designed to analyse existing partnerships, we find it has practical implications in deciding where and how to invest time and resources. The different dimensions have no priority over each other, but, taken together, they provide a comprehensive approach to describing the closeness of two organisations.

One of the key insights from Boschma is that on each of these dimensions, it is possible to be both too close and too far. Taking social proximity as an example, if the distance here is too large, then it is likely that the two parties will struggle to build effective relationships because there is not a shared understanding between the individuals involved. If, however, the people in question are too close in their social ties, sharing a common educational background, for example, this too may hamper innovation. A business conducted on family ties, or old school connections, to the exclusion of other potential dimensions of social relationship, may be less effective.

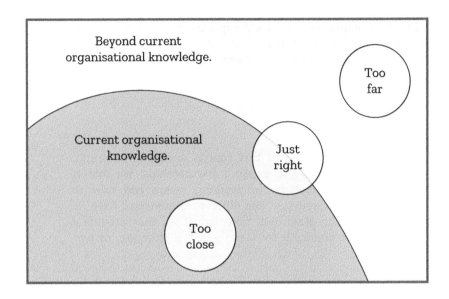

Figure 6: Balancing proximity in partnerships.

You can use proximity as a tool to help build your partnerships and for understanding how to build social capital. To put this in context, concentrating on partnering with the world's best, even though they are 10,000 kilometres and several time zones away, might be 'mindlessly global'. The common trap here is to focus only on cognitive proximity, when you may find other world-leading partners closer to you who can deliver equal impact with less. The other extreme is to be 'hopelessly local' – partnering with what you find on your doorstep, but not really considering other possibilities.

Using these five dimensions, Table 11 illustrates in more detail what too close and too far looks like in each of these dimensions.

TOO CLOSE	DIMENSION	TOO FAR
Many individuals in the company have a very similar technical knowledge base to the university team.	**Cognitive proximity**	None of the company team share a common technical language with any of the university team.
Rigid, formal, and highly orchestrated meetings and engagements.	**Organisational proximity**	Random, poorly coordinated sessions. No actions agreed or follow-ups.
Company staff are heavily involved in mutual social and friendship groups with key university staff.	**Social proximity**	Poor levels of social rapport. Low levels of warmth and social connection.
Danger of conflicts of interest or bending rules from funding bodies.	**Institutional proximity**	Basic misunderstanding of legal frameworks. Endemic misunderstandings.
Danger of cultural narrowness.	**Geographical proximity**	Almost impossible to create any real connections and partnership.

Table 11: Proximity matrix.

In the following list are indications of what an ideal level of proximity is for each of these dimensions.

- *Cognitive proximity.* Some of the individuals in the partner organisations have a similar technical knowledge base. The diversity in technical fields becomes a source of innovation strength.
- *Organisational proximity.* Both partners have a clear idea of how to run mutual activities, respecting different approaches to flexibility and actions.
- *Social proximity.* Mutually respectful, friendly, and professional. Friendships are used to support partnership and build a more strategic relationship.
- *Institutional proximity.* There is a clear understanding in both parties of differences and a common desire to overcome structural differences.
- *Geographical proximity.* There is a mutual understanding of what needs to be done to mitigate any potential issues associated with geographical distance through easy-to-implement ways of working.

It is important to stress that there are specific things that you can do to mitigate either overly close or overly distant positioning on the dimensions. The most important thing in the first instance is to honestly map out the situation and then identify the highest priority issue to resolve. There is an interconnectivity between each of these dimensions, and therefore as the situation in one dimension begins to resolve, some of the other dimensions will also likely improve.

When it comes to who to build strategic partnerships with, considering all five elements of proximity holistically is an important element of knowing where to invest time and energy. You can invest a number of years in building a partnership, and those occupying a combination of difficult proximal positions may struggle to become strategic partnerships. At the same time, be careful when making assumptions about what is 'too close' and 'too far'. Some of your strategic partners will be located in different continents, and in different time zones, but technology is helping to mitigate any negative influences of geographical distance.

21.
ALIGNING CAPABILITIES AND OUTCOMES

Perhaps the most natural way for a researcher from a company to discuss a potential research project with an academic is in terms of a set of common research outcomes. These are the specific knowledge outputs that both partners imagine may be produced during the course of the project. In this type of project, negotiations will likely focus on the timelines involved in generating the outcomes, payment milestones, other resources required for success, and the allocation of any intellectual property (IP) that is created during the project.

For an ad hoc project with a university, it is hard to avoid aligning a company interest and an academic interest like this. However, there are risks in this approach for longer projects. It assumes that the priorities of both parties will remain stable throughout the entire project, that their mutual interest in the outcomes will remain high, and that the key people required for the project do not change their roles. These factors will almost inevitably be more variable for a company than a university. Whereas a university might be comfortable waiting three or four years for a PhD student to answer a research question, at a company, business priorities can change much more rapidly than that, which can lead to a misalignment of desired outcomes over the same time frame.

If you plan to create a larger and more strategic partnership with a university, then simply scaling-up the outcome alignment approach above can create significant issues.

A more robust approach for larger-scale partnerships is to try and shift the focus away from specific research outcomes and towards the common capabilities that will have enduring importance for both the company and the university. For example, a company may have a keen commercial interest in the development of a family of new chemical materials that are able to deliver a step-change increase in the energy density of an electric storage device over that of current lithium ion batteries. This interest could be reflected in sponsored research projects on specific classes of materials. Alternatively, the partnership may be recast as a way for the company and university to co-invest in unique computational and experimental techniques that can discover compositions of matter that deliver multiple desirable properties (cost, bulk density, safety, environmental sustainability, energy density, etc.). For the university, these techniques can be used to deliver a stream of publishable results on new materials, and for the company they can be used to discover new and patentable materials. Crucially, there is now no need to expect that the specific materials discovered by the academic team are in any way related to those discovered by the company team.

This approach is a very efficient way to translate state-of-the-art academic work into a competitive advantage for an industrial company.

In a research alignment model you will typically pay for access to the IP arising from the research, as well as time and resources required for the project. Under the capabilities model, you will focus on creating a sustainable investment and staffing model, a joint strategic direction, and access to capability, as opposed to the control of arising IP.

Aligning around a capability will focus your attention on the initial shape and set-up of a programme of work, the ongoing access arrangements, and agreeing plans for developing those shared capabilities. If projects are aligned by outcome *only*, all the outcomes must be defined in advance. Under the capability model, individual projects do not necessarily need to be highly aligned in outcome and a wide range of potential outcomes becomes possible. The investment that the company makes is in shared and open capability. This in turn is attractive to local and national government funding bodies.

We have found over the past 20 years that high-impact co-created capabilities will often have the following attributes:

- *Specialised space:* This is NOT office space, nor is it a 'Google Lab' type environment – an office space with deckchairs. It could be a chemistry lab; class II bio-lab; radio-chemistry lab; robotic engineering machine hall; darkened imaging space; electronics fabrication lab; operating theatre; clean-room; virtual reality cave; data centre; pilot plant hall; cell imaging lab; or neuroscience lab.
- *Differentiated equipment:* This is NOT off-the-shelf low-value equipment. It could be HT synthesis robots; plate readers; robotic arm; TEM; micro-manipulator; surface coater; precision 3D printer; laser etching; parallel computer; specialised mixers, spray dryers, and pilot scale lines; specialised testing kit; fMRI; femto-second laser; or SAXS beamline.
- *Differentiated methodology and software platforms:* This is NOT enterprise software packages. It could be measurement techniques; sample preparation methods; new assays; algorithms; simulation operating system; adaptive experimental design; microbial assays; modelling platforms; bespoke Python/R scripts; bioinformatics pipelines. Often the methods can be trade secrets and know-how rather than patents.
- *Skilled technical support staff:* These are NOT junior academic staff. They are a repository of specialised expertise and hands-on innovators. They provide a flexible and deployable staff for partners to work with.
- *Network of hi-tech equipment and service providers:* These providers understand that the facility is both a customer of their services AND a means to drive innovation for them.

- *Academic and scientific thought leaders:* In the university these are the premier-league professors with world-class reputations, a proven track record of winning large competitive grants, and an ambition to be the best.
- *Professional management and business engagement:* Real understanding of technical capability and the needs of commercial organisations.

This framework was co-created with leading academics and professional services staff at the University of Liverpool over the past 15 years; for this reason we call it the Liverpool Model.

The shift that occurs when you focus on capabilities is to move conversations up a level from the outcomes for a single, more tactical project, towards operational goals focusing on what both parties will be investing to create and sustain a unique capability. Once the concept of capability alignment has been established, the next stages of developing this alignment are reasonably intuitive. As the focus shifts away from research alignment to capability alignment, new opportunities appear. In particular, it becomes fruitful to ask what other capabilities could be built with the university that you had not previously considered. Figure 7 compares outcome-only and capability alignment. In an outcome-only alignment, the capability bases of the university and company remain non-overlapped. The work involved in creating alignment needs to articulate how the capabilities will be brought together within the confines of a particular project to achieve a commonly agreed outcome. In a capability alignment approach, the work involved in creating alignment involves identification of the overlapping requirements of both partners prior to a particular project starting. This allows important issues such as access, arising IP, payment terms, and management to be addressed up front. Outcomes will tend to emerge as a consequence of the initial alignment effort, and the close ongoing working arrangements.

All collaborative projects between a company and a university are dependent for their success on the quality and complementarity of the capabilities that each organisation can mobilise, and the degree of alignment they can achieve towards a set of common targets. Where the innovation capabilities in a company and a university are not pre-aligned or overlapping, each collaborative project that is set up needs explicit up-front work to create alignment. Where there is a shared innovation capability between the company and university, a very wide range of projects is possible. On a project-by-project basis, there is then no need for up-front alignment on outcomes. The differences between these two approaches to alignment are illustrated in Figure 7.

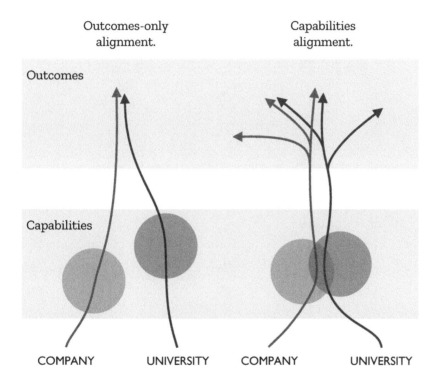

Figure 7: Research outcome vs capability alignment.

22.
MANAGING RELATIONSHIPS

Here we focus on the human–human interfaces and the role that relationship managers can play in closing the gap between individuals and organisations.

One of the most important sources of value creation in a knowledge-based organisation such as your team is the ability to build 'social capital' across partnerships.

Social capital (Nahapiet and Ghoshal 1998) refers to *the sum of all the actual and potential resources embedded within a partnership*, including aspects such as knowledge (what people know), attitudes (what people think), networks (who people know), and resources (what people have). This type of capital arises from the network of relationships that an organisation creates and maintains. It is a valuable resource. Organisations that have learnt how to mobilise it can create significant strategic benefits for both themselves and their partners. For some companies, it can become a unique source of competitive advantage. We describe some dimensions of social capital in the table below.

DIMENSION	MEANING
Network ties	Who you know affects what you know.
Network configuration	Where your network reaches to affects the quality of the network.
Appropriable organisation	Benefiting from the social networks formed for other reasons.
Shared codes and language	These directly lower the barriers to forming social networks.
Shared narratives	Beyond a shared language, stories and metaphors create shared meaning.
Trust	A belief in the good intent, competence, reliability, and openness of a partner.
Norms	The basis for consensus in a social system.
Obligations	A commitment to undertake an activity in the future.
Identification	Seeing oneself as one with another group.

Table 12: The different dimensions of social capital.

Each of these dimensions adds to the value of social capital.

Network ties are the means by which your extended network gives you access to information that is often privileged, and very often available sooner than it is available to others. The network provides a low-cost way to harvest referrals from existing networks to new contacts. The exact configuration of your network means that even relatively loose ties within your network can stretch a long way and are often quite efficient means for information sharing and information gathering.

Professional-body memberships, friendship groups, shared work experiences in other organisations, and shared educational experiences are all organisational contexts that can be appropriated and used as the kernels for new networks and social capital.

Shared codes, language, and narratives are powerful forms of social capital. Shared codes of behaviour and shared language develop over time. The process of forming these shared means of communicating are powerful means to create social capital. When partners begin to create and recount a set of shared stories, it shows that a high level of social capital has been created.

Within the context of partnerships, the idea of trust is multidi-mensional. As the level of social capital increases, trust will extend beyond basic interpersonal trust to include organi-sational trust. This type of trust is hard to quantify, but it becomes evident in the quality of interactions between the two organisations.

High levels of social capital are built on a broad consensus, or set of norms, that indicate a shared willingness to value diversity and openness between the partners, and that also includes a tolerance for failure.

Social capital leads to a shared sense of mutual obligation. This is forward looking and is based on expectations of shared future activity. Note that this type of obligation is explicitly not a legal obligation, but rather something that arises from the other elements of social capital. Reputationally binding obligations are examples of this type of social capital.

In a mature partnership, with a high level of social capital, a sense of mutual identification emerges. The partnership itself becomes an identifiable thing, over and above the individual identity of the constituent organisations. This element of social capital is a major source of motivation for partners to work together and combine knowledge and assets.

▶◀

Social capital is shared by all the parties to a relationship. It is an emergent property of the innovation ecosystem. Social capital cannot confer exclusive ownership or benefits for an individual organisation because it comes from social exchange and its development requires ways of working that strengthen relationships. The creation and maintenance of social capital for a company is therefore one of the most critical ways to view relationship management with strategic partners.

Each partner you work with has a potential to deliver an incredibly rich extended network and set of resources from which your company can benefit. However, to generate this value, you will be required to play a role linking and bridging, closing the gaps that exist between your company and its partners. This could be by understanding and identifying the operational constraints, language, norms, and values of a key partner, or perhaps understanding which networks your partner has access to, and the codes and values that govern their behaviour.

For many tough-minded commercial innovators, social capital will sound like a soft concept. In reality, it is a way of describing something that is both hard to create and manage, and of enormous commercial value if it is properly exploited. Because social capital is non-transferable, it is less easy to value than more concrete and mobile forms of capital (IP, equipment, cash), but it has some unique and uniquely attractive qualities. It is this non-transferability that allows social capital to confer such significant competitive advantage – the productive relationship you cultivate with a university cannot be 'copied' by a competitor and its existence doesn't reduce the amount of time it would take to reproduce elsewhere. Investment in social capital, if done carefully, creates soft power that will last considerably longer than the equivalent outlay on a hard asset.

The building of social capital within a strategic partnership also leads to a positive feedback loop. There is a virtuous circle created: the bigger the fund of social capital, the bigger and better the projects that can be tackled. Success in these bigger partnership projects then creates even more social capital.

We have made a conscious decision here not to discuss in detail the numerous collaborative structures that are possible between multiple partners, e.g. joint ventures, strategic alliances, affiliations, coalitions, and consortia. In our experience, it is difficult and high-risk to try and create complex consortia and alliances without having any pre-existing relationships.

23.
THE RELATIONSHIP MANAGER

The development of an in-depth partnership requires a professional approach to partner management for long-term sustainability. Usually, the best way to achieve this is to have an individual in the company who is responsible for managing the development of the relationship with the university partner. This is rarely a full-time position; it will often be part of a person's role and would often complement an R&D leader who was driving a particular project with the university partner. A relationship manager would not usually be involved in technical reviews of ongoing projects. Typically this person's role would include:

- Preparing for formal meetings between partners. This may include creating the agenda, reviewing actions, and deciding on the strategic discussions and decisions to be addressed at the meetings.
- Periodically checking for the quality of strategic alignment between the two organisations and initiatives that lead to identification of new opportunities such as deep dives on differentiated capabilities and/or technologies.
- Checking the pace and rhythm of the partnership across its full breadth.
- Resolving any issues raised within the partnership.
- Periodic analysis of the project portfolio and, if required, recommendations for how to evolve the portfolio.
- Exploration of new opportunities for collaboration and new ways of working.

To increase social capital, a relationship manager needs to play a role in linking an organisation's internal networks and cultures with external networks and cultures. You could think of it as someone who is maintaining the appropriate levels of proximity between partners in order for social capital to develop (e.g. being on the same or a similar page in terms of values, knowledge, and organisational cultures).

While a specific relationship manager may have formal responsibility for this type of work, the nature of R&D today means that, to a degree, everyone has some responsibility for this as part of their role. Typical 'formal' responsibilities include:

- Improving knowledge management.
- Increasing external visibility.
- Providing internal co-ordination.
- Helping to eliminate accountability and intervention problems (e.g. taking a lead in resolving issues that are to do with how the company as a whole works with the university).
- Offering a focal point for communication and exchange (e.g. setting up regular weekly or fortnightly calls with their opposite number).
- Development of strategic legal agreement portfolios and other arrangements.
- Professionally winding down or closing a partnership.

A key aspect of building social capital is that a relationship manager will often work in spaces where they do not control all the resources that flow into the relationship. Nor will they have accountability or responsibility for all the decisions that are made that may affect the relationship. That said, relationship managers will often be the 'face of the company' within the university and as such will often have to navigate through tricky situations and give 'bad news' while maintaining the social capital that has been built.

This type of role raises challenges associated with managing without power. The task therefore demands a high degree of sophistication in terms of both interpersonal skills (communicating with people effectively) and emotional intelligence (understanding what people want and why they act the way they do). Without these qualities to draw upon, people involved in or leading the development of strategic partnerships will not be equipped to successfully manage the myriad situations that can and do arise.

There are some structured tools available to help in this situation and we recommend that you consider carefully where responsibility (whose work plan does the task full under), accountability (who pays), and influence (whose opinion matters) rest within the organisation. It is important, also, to be aware of the basis of your authority and the authority of others. Max Weber's tripartite of authority can be readily adapted to these situations, with *charismatic authority* coming from the individual, *hierarchical authority* bestowed from the traditional structures of an organisation, and *professional authority* arising from peer-to-peer recognition of knowledge and qualifications (Weber 1978/1922). The balance of these bases of authority is radically different in companies and universities. In companies, it is often the individual within the role (charismatic + hierarchical) who dominates the ability to control activities, while in a university these are suppressed in deference to professional credentials.

The other fundamental challenge that a relationship manager will face is that organisations do not stand still while they establish how to work together. You cannot simply stop the cogs from turning. A relationship manager will therefore need to create, embody, and scope out a kind of gearing system that enables the two organisations to form a partnership while they are still moving. An understanding of the 'clockspeed' of the university and the specific company is essential in achieving this. The term arises from the concept of the cycle times that are inherent within organisations (Fine 1999). It can be measured in anything from days to years and typically refers to the elapsed time between releases of products and services. All universities have a strong annual cycle, with a yearly tick-rate built into both their internal processes and those of the institutions around them (e.g. funding bodies). Companies, on the other hand, can take anything from three years to release new products in the automotive sector to weekly updates of an application program interface (API) in a digital service business. Prepare yourself to be surprised at how quickly a university can complete some tasks and their slowness in other areas when compared to your own business.

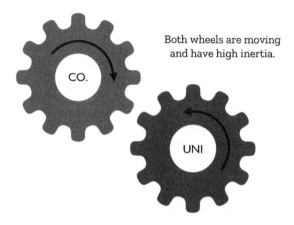

Both wheels are moving and have high inertia.

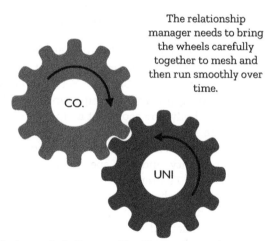

The relationship manager needs to bring the wheels carefully together to mesh and then run smoothly over time.

Figure 8: The clockspeed challenge of building relationship capital.

Once aligned, the manager will need to oil the partnership cogs to ensure that things are moving and stay in alignment. To do this well they will need to understand the culture and foibles of their own company, including typical behaviours, the way the company does things, and how they perceive, reflect on, and talk about their challenges, alongside the culture of the organisation that the company is partnering with. Sometimes a relationship manager will only find out the nature of the other organisation through making mistakes. Reflection, empathy, and a commitment to adapting how they work is therefore always important.

In 2008, the Princeton scholar Dr. Emily Pronin published a wonderful short paper called 'How We See Ourselves and How We See Others' (Pronin 2008). In this review paper, Pronin summarises more than 40 years of psychological research on the origin and effects of the differences that exist between perceiving oneself versus perceiving others. The abstract of her review describes the issues:

> People see themselves differently from how they see others. They are immersed in their own sensations, emotions, and cognitions at the same time that their experience of others is dominated by what can be observed externally. This basic asymmetry has broad consequences. It leads people to judge themselves and their own behavior differently from how they judge others and those others' behavior. Often, those differences produce disagreement and conflict.

The paper concludes that 'individuals can be mindful that it is not only their own behaviour that is sensitive to the constraints of the situation, but others as well. Perhaps this could prompt them to show more charity when others fail to meet expectations'.

Relationship managers, both with formal roles and those who find themselves managing a relationship as part of a wider role, need to create space to learn how to work in a partnership. But even with training and experience, a relationship manager will sometimes leave a meeting feeling misunderstood. They need to constantly check what language works, and how to present things in a way that resonates authentically with their partners. This requires creativity and patience.

24.
LEADERSHIP

The company you work for may have an explicit leadership model that you can look to as a guide for thinking about the personal skills and qualities needed to build social capital in a strategic partnership. However, many organisations will not have a specific leadership model, or the model may not be set up to help those company staff who are actively trying to manage one or more innovation partnerships. We have found that the transformational leadership model provides a good framework for the professional development needs of those in R&D who need to learn how to manage partnerships (Burns 1978). It also distinguishes between transactional management styles that focus on the outputs of the interaction and a values-based approach that utilises the goals and resources of the people involved.

We have summarised some key elements of this model, which are most relevant in leading partnerships.

- *Focus:* A transformational leadership model focuses on the needs of team members other than the leader. This means that a transformational leader will spend time on the needs of the organisation, and his or her behaviour is designed to try and build a broad-based commitment towards the objectives of the organisation.

- *Culture:* Transformational leadership also focuses on organisational culture. This is not about changing the culture of their organisation or that of the partner's organisation. They are working within the status quo to achieve a result. This means a leader needs to understand the culture of both their own organisation and the culture of their partner organisation.
- *Vision led:* Transformational leaders build a compelling vision for the future of the partnership. From this comes clear goals that individuals can stretch to achieve.
- *Non-management:* Transactional leadership styles emphasise the use of management techniques, including compliance, structure, hierarchy, tasks, rewards, and punishment. Transformational leadership relies much less on these approaches and in contrast relies on empowerment and inspiration to get teams of people to work together to achieve a goal.
- *Resilience:* Leaders involved in partnership management need to actively build their own well-being and resilience. These leaders develop emotional intelligence so they can take feedback, manage their own mood and motivations, and build empathy for others.

Working in a partnership is not a straightforward commercial transactional arrangement. You must consider the organisation you are partnering with in detail, listening to their priorities, the pressures that they are under, and the people that they are accountable to. In any productive partnership there is give and take, but you must understand your partner's priorities beyond just your relationship to understand where these lines should be drawn. The same is also true of your partner.

One way of framing this is to think in terms of the following simple questions:

- What is good for me (my career, my department, my company)?
- What is good for my partner (their careers, departments, university)?
- What is good for both of us (our shared vision, strategy, and projects)?
- What is good for the wider innovation ecosystem (the needs of other stakeholders, funders, citizens, and consumers)?

Ideally the answers to these questions will be aligned, but often they are not, and steps are needed to reframe problems, understand issues, and negotiate differences to move forward.

25.
USING FORMAL AGREEMENTS

Formal legal agreements can help stipulate the arrangements that need to be in place to foster ongoing access to resources, workspace, and knowledge. In this section, we present a framework for these agreements, highlighting the key components that should be agreed between you and the partner.

Formal legal agreements provide an overarching framework for a portfolio of different individual contract types, relationships, and consortia arrangements. In one-off activities with a university, such as contract research or a PhD studentship, the risks are best managed within a single stand-alone legal contract. In consortia arrangements, for example where a large third-party funder is involved, the legal framework will largely be set by the funder of the scheme. However, should the partnership mature, you will need a framework that not only draws all the different projects and capacities together into one coherent approach, but also articulates the mutual understanding between your company and the university. Elements of this type of agreement may not be legally binding. Nonetheless these agreements can help to formalise ongoing arrangements for access to capabilities (i.e. equipment, buildings, data processing capabilities), encourage synergy across work streams, and introduce new, more balanced approaches to publication, intellectual property (IP) rights, and confidentiality.

TYPE OF ACTIVITY	LEGAL AGREEMENT
Letter of support	A bespoke letter expressing formal support from the company for a university-led project proposal. It is normally written so as not to be a legally binding agreement and may include co-funding estimates.
Confidential disclosure	Covers a disclosure of information from one party to another. The information disclosed is to be held by the receiving party in confidence for an agreed time and covering a specific subject matter.
Consultancy	A simple commercial contract for desk work done by a university expert. Will include a confidentiality clause, hourly or daily fee rates, and output milestones.
Fees for service	A simple commercial contract for work done by the university team. Will include a confidentiality clause, a per-sample fee rate, and output or reporting milestones.
Heads of terms	A non-binding document that outlines the main issues that are relevant to a potential legal agreement.
Company-sponsored research	A project fully funded by the company to undertake specific research activity that will be carried out by university staff and exploiting university lab space and know-how.
Grant-funded research	This is a co-funded activity in which the state funding body would expect to see the creation of something for the public good as well as specific results and outputs for the company.

Table 13: Examples of typical interactions and legal contracts required.

There is a portfolio of different types of agreement that are commonly used to manage a specific interaction or project between a company and a university. It is helpful to understand the legal status of these various agreements.

Very often, the slowest part of a contract negotiation between a company and university will be around IP and intellectual property rights (IPR). There are various IPR allocation and access options that can be agreed by a company and a university. The options that are used will depend on a variety of factors, including specific national or regional policies, the university's own status, statutes, policies, and the relative importance of the project to the company.

It may be more appropriate for the university to control the results or for the company to control results, to have immediate exclusivity or time-limited exclusivity, or it may be best not to patent the results of a project at all – but to publish. Some of the terminology used within the context of IPR in legal agreements includes:

- *Access rights (also known as licences).* These confer a legal right to use, sell, reproduce, further develop, and otherwise commercially exploit an innovation. It may be that a party requires only some access rights and does not need to own an innovation. Access rights may be non-exclusive or exclusive.
- *Intellectual property rights (IPR).* Patents, design rights, copyright, trademarks, know-how/trade secrets, and other comparable legal rights.
- *Licence.* The grant of permission to access an innovation for various purposes. See 'access rights' above.
- *Ownership.* The controller of the IPR in an innovation controls which parties can commercially use or manufacture an innovation protected by that right.

TYPE OF ACTIVITY	IP ALLOCATION
Letter of support	None.
Confidential disclosure	None.
Consultancy	Advisory output that only very rarely includes arising IP, as no practical work is performed. Usually the specific advice will be held confidentially by the company as it may lead to commercial advantage.
Fees for service	The company will normally control the resulting data with any arising IP assigned to the company. Any method improvements made in delivering the service will usually be owned by the university.
Heads of terms	A heads of terms normally includes reference to the management of IP in a project, but until a full legal contract is signed, the obligations in the document will not be legally binding.
Company-sponsored research	Where companies pay all the costs, they may expect to exclusively control any arising IP. A university will often include provisions for the company to pay the university to access the background IP.
Grant-funded research	Where some costs are covered by grant bodies and universities, the university usually controls the arising IP, with some pre-agreed provisions for licensing this IP to the company.

Table 14: Examples of typical interactions and IP allocations required.

Examples of typical interactions and contracts needed include letters of support, confidentiality disclosure agreements, consultancy arrangements, and research agreements (as shown in Table 14). In each of these we find a range of default positions on IP allocation. Where a company pays a university a set fee for a service such as those provided within a lab or facility, the arrangements can typically be covered by a contract template in which the default position is that the company will control the data, but any improvements in method will be held by the university.

Note that the quadrant model we discussed in Section 4 leads directly to a range of IP models. The best way to accelerate discussions with universities around the IP parts of contracts is to be crystal clear about which of these boxes you are in. The implications for a university of negotiating a service-fee-based contract versus a discovery-type contract are substantial.

26.
STRATEGIC PARTNERSHIP AGREEMENTS

Creating a formal agreement for a strategic partnership requires a model that reflects the approaches that we have discussed throughout this playbook. One of the benefits of such an agreement is to help to reduce the legal overheads of project-by-project contracts. They reduce the transaction costs of having the legal, research, and finance teams of both organisations repeatedly negotiating and renegotiating terms and conditions each time you want to collaborate on a project or programme. Lengthy negotiations such as these can be a barrier to working effectively with your partners over time.

Overarching or umbrella frameworks enable you to share problems more openly with a university partner and help you to start projects more quickly. If they are used well, they are an excellent tool for supporting the development of social capital. You will also find that if the partnership with the university has matured and sustained over time, there is a lot more going on under the radar that hasn't been articulated or captured within the formal project by project contracts. Formalising this activity through a written agreement can help protect the university and leave it less vulnerable to changes in company personnel.

We do not recommend negotiating such agreements when first developing a partnership. These arrangements are built on trust and experience between two organisations that have already been working together effectively on multiple projects over a period of time.

The framework presented here is the best practice we have observed. It is as simple as we can make it, and it should only be a starting point for negotiations with a university partner. We do not include any legal clauses, as you will need to identify the specific clauses that will be required for different legal jurisdictions and with individual universities. For example, intellectual property (IP) considerations will vary considerably in different legal jurisdictions. The default position on academic ownership and licensing varies from country to country, and the implications of public funding and state aid will be country or region specific.

Experience has shown that trying to create a single comprehensive legal agreement to manage all aspects of a strategic partnership between a company and a university is a difficult approach to take. It requires the legal teams of the company and the university to try to imagine all possible outcomes (good, bad, and middling) of a large number of very different types of interaction between two complex organisations over three or five years. The approach we suggest uses three elements to provide clarity:

- Joint statement of endeavour.
- Preliminary discussions.
- Portfolio of agreements.

Together, these help to guide how the strategic aims of the partnership are managed and how the operational mechanisms work, as well as how individual projects executed at a tactical level are managed and run. We recognise that each prospective partnership will sit within a different context, and this will be reflected in the agreements.

The joint statement of endeavour is a document that needs to be drafted by lawyers and will be signed by both parties, but it is explicitly NOT legally binding except for the provisions that cover the mutual disclosure of confidential information. This agreement operates at the tip of the iceberg and is essentially a manifesto for the alliance. It is mainly required to manage the strategic relationship between the company and the university as corporate entities and the risks that arise in the partnership as a whole. A template for creating a joint statement of endeavour (JSE) is shown towards the end of this section. Note that a JSE is not the same thing as a heads of terms. Although both documents have in common the fact that they are not legally binding, a heads of terms is only a transitory document that is used to frame a legally binding agreement, after which the heads are then discarded. A JSE, on the other hand, is intended to have a long-term impact on the way two organisations work together.

Preliminary discussions about potential areas of interest or specific challenges are an important part of how collaborations develop. These discussions are the lifeblood of a healthy strategic partnership and therefore finding a way to make them as easy as possible is well worth doing. Sharing information that you feel is private and valuable is a good way to build trust and relationships. However, when sharing company information with another party, it is vital that this will not expose either you or your company to risk or reputational damage.

The preliminary discussions section of the JSE defines what confidential information is and also how it can be securely shared in a preliminary discussion. A preliminary discussion clause is one of the highest value aspects of a JSE-type agreement as it lowers any nervousness regarding IP in initial discussions. As part of this clause, it is also helpful to articulate what isn't confidential. For example:

- Information that is already in the public domain.
- Where something has been developed independently of the information received.
- Information that comes via a third party.
- Information that is required by law to be disclosed if requested.

Preliminary discussions are to be encouraged. They are the basis of how new ideas and projects can be created between the company and the university. Company scientists and project leaders need to be confident that the initial ideas they are sharing with university staff can be kept confidential. As a conversation progresses from initial meetings held under these 'preliminary discussion' arrangements, one or both of the parties may start to feel uncomfortable about sharing any more information. At this point, it is possible to put in place a more specific confidential disclosure agreement (CDA) with a well-defined scope and for a well-defined purpose. This approach encourages as many preliminary conversations to happen as possible, while ensuring that very specific and detailed confidential data and information can be protected by the party that owns it.

SECTION	DESCRIPTION
Purpose	The purpose and what it builds on. Who it is between and how long it will be in place for.
Principles	A statement of the shared principles that parties recognise as critical to strategic collaboration.
Governance	The arrangements set up to manage the relationship, built on openness and trust.
Escalation	A process for how to resolve more serious issues that may arise.
Agreement portfolio	The portfolio of standardised agreements that will be used for specific types of project.
Public statements	How the university and company talk publicly about their partnership with mutual consent.
Law and jurisdiction	The jurisdiction(s) in which the agreement will be valid.

Table 15: Non-legally binding content of a joint statement of endeavour (JSE).

As can be seen in Table 15, the bulk of a JSE is deliberately about the aspects that will not be covered by future legal agreements in the portfolio. The principles behind the partnership sit at the highest level and make clear the value of undertaking projects that are scientifically and commercially interesting to the highest standards, with ethical integrity. They may set out the aspiration for a culture of openness and transparency between the two organisations and their stakeholders, and demonstrate a recognition of the need for confidentiality to foster creativity and trust.

The governance of routine workflows and escalation procedures for conflict resolution form the more practical expectations of the partnership. The purpose and membership of governance boards may be defined, for example, providing strategic oversight of the partnership, including engagement with external stakeholders, prioritising opportunities, or sharing information on potential collaborations. Together these elements of the JSE recognise agreed positions and processes for any challenges that might arise from different organisational cultures and constraints.

The agreement portfolio includes templates that are each legally binding, and the specific way that IP rights (IPR) are dealt with in these agreements is described in Section 25 (Using Formal Agreements). These might include:

- Materials transfer agreement (MTA).
- Confidential disclosure agreement (CDA).
- Consultancy.
- Services.
- Sponsored research.
- PhD studentships.

While a JSE is often a non-legally binding agreement, when it is signed by two mature organisations, they effectively create a reputationally binding partnership.

In a strategic partnership it becomes useful to create a comprehensive portfolio of contract templates and backbones. One way to develop a complete portfolio is to define two classes of contractual documents.

The first is a *contract template*. If both the university and the company believe the whole contract can be resolved once and for all in a universally applicable way, it means that individual projects that use this template can be set up without any further negotiation. This type of agreement is a fully formed legal contract that can be signed as it is. It is like a cake that has already been made.

The second type of document is a *contract backbone.* If a whole contract cannot easily be resolved in a comprehensive way, then it is very often possible to agree everything except the more controversial or slower-to-resolve issues (the bottlenecks). In these cases, it is useful to agree between the company and the university a contract backbone. This is not a full legal agreement. It lacks some important parts of the contract and cannot be signed without further work. This is like a cake pre-mix; it needs more ingredients to be added, and more work, before it is ready.

Very often, discussions around IPR will focus on patents, which are the most recognisable form of IP protection, and the associated rights for an invention. However, contrary to popular misconception, a patent does NOT give a company or person the right to do something; it only gives them the right to EXCLUDE others from doing it. Equally, concepts of ownership can be misleading. If in doubt, make sure you understand who has access to the assets you care about and who can control this access.

Company innovators often make the mistake of assuming that a formally signed legal agreement between their company and another organisation is primarily a legal matter. Nothing could be further from the truth. Although these agreements are encoded in appropriate legalese, and they require the specialised skills of your legal advisors to draft and edit, they are always primarily about enabling great innovation to happen. It is your responsibility as a company innovator to clearly articulate the business intent behind any agreement that you ask your legal teams to draft. Your aim in making a strategic partnership agreement with a university is to facilitate bigger and better innovation opportunities than are otherwise possible, while keeping an eye on managing the risks.

Formal agreements and joint statements of endeavour play an important role in providing an overarching framework for different individual contract types, relationships, and consortia arrangements. Using a layered structure such as the one described here can help provide clarity about the strategic aims of the partnership and the operational elements, as well as how individual projects are executed. It can also help you to get IP and confidentiality agreements in place that are appropriate to the level of risk associated with an activity or arrangement. Fundamentally, formal agreements help to create a more stable basis on which to build a strategic partnership. They are often used to codify what is already in place, leaving these activities less vulnerable to changes in personnel. They can also form a basis for maturing partnerships, helping to reduce transaction costs and putting in place a stable basis from which to build.

27.
WORKING IN PARTNERSHIP

In this section, we focus on some simple techniques for bringing people together. We look at workshops you could use to foster co-creation around shared problems, surface some of the assumptions your company staff and university staff may bring to the partnership, and provide some initial guidance on confidentiality.

Partnerships are very different to friendships. This may sound obvious, but we know from our experience that it is very easy to lose sight of this. As you are not working with friends, you need to avoid things feeling too 'cosy' and muddying the waters – losing sight of the organisational priorities you are delivering against. You must, at the same time, keep informal channels open, to keep listening and learning, and to be authentic. There is a tightrope here that you must walk.

Co-creating a common language, understanding, and ways of working between organisations is essential. You must sit down very early in the process to thrash out the specific goals that partners are looking to achieve and identify areas of commonality, synergy, and potential exchange. Even where there is such a thing as 'common language', people can still have different assumptions about what that language means.

From a company point of view, you may see a joint project as being underpinned with a contract, payments, milestones, and outcomes. For the university, these words can mean different things. A contract may be seen as an agreement, a payment as a grant or stipend, and milestones are sometimes viewed as progress steps. These differences in interpretation are not uniform across the university sector, but the dominant cultural assumptions made by universities as institutions often lead to different expectations.

COMMERCIAL DOMAIN		UNIVERSITY DOMAIN
Contract	→	Agreement
Payment	→	Grant
Milestone	→	Progress
Delivery	→	Research

Table 16: Common language masking different assumptions.

One area where the differences in professional culture between universities and companies is most apparent is around disclosure and confidentiality. As a company employee, whenever you share information with a third party, you are acting on behalf of the company. Therefore, when you write an email to a senior manager in the university, it is your responsibility to ensure that you have not shared anything that is confidential. Trust doesn't come into it. You may trust the people you are working with and the information, but you may well be breaching your employment contract if you acted otherwise.

The culture in universities is different in that interpersonal trust does come into the picture. Quite often you will find that a university manager will share something with you that is shared with you personally, in confidence. Say for example, the university is about to announce a €10M investment in a new Life Sciences facility, you may receive an email with the information, but may be asked not to share it. This typically means 'do not share', even within your own organisation. The implication is that this information is not for everyone in the company, but it is for you personally. As the university's main contact with your company, it has been shared with you, outside a legal confidentiality agreement, to help you work more effectively with the university. The information will allow you to be aware of specific challenges being faced or opportunities on the horizon. This may make you feel uncomfortable.

Given the professional culture within a company, there are two default responses to this situation that do not work well for partnership building. The first is a defence response, which is to say to the university that they cannot share this information with you. Often this is impractical as you simply don't know when a piece of confidential information is going to be disclosed. Furthermore, even if it was practical, we wouldn't advise this approach as it places an unnecessary barrier between you and the partner. University staff and academics need to see that they have a relationship with you personally, as well as with the company. The second response would be to share the information more widely within the company. For reasons discussed above, this would be a breach of the confidence entrusted to you.

It is important, therefore, that you know the limits of what you can and cannot do with the information that has been shared. While each circumstance should be considered on its own merits, there are a few rules of thumb to go by. First, once you have received a piece of information that is confidential, take some time to reflect on it. What are the implications of this information for your company? Which other departments might it affect? What, if anything, have you been asked to do with the information? How long should the information remain confidential? If it helps, it may be a good idea to discuss the situation with a trusted colleague within your company, without sharing the specific information.

Depending on your answers to these questions, so long as the information that has been shared with you doesn't create any form of moral hazard, it is important that you take every step to ensure it is not compromised. If there is another department within your company that you feel this intelligence would be crucial for, it is perfectly reasonable to return to your contact at the university and ask for their permission to share the information with that department, outlining your reasons why. Also, as part of managing your relationships with the university and helping them understand the constraints that you are working under, it is also perfectly reasonable to share some of the constraints around confidentiality agreements.

When building relationships with your university partners, you will continually find that fine judgement is needed about how to switch between off- and on-the-record conversations. One device that you might like to consider using in your meetings and workshops is the Chatham House Rule. This originated at Chatham House in London, UK, with the aim of providing anonymity to speakers and to encourage openness and the sharing of information. It is now used throughout the world as an aid to free discussion.

> When a meeting, or part thereof, is held under the Chatham House Rule, participants are free to use the information received, but neither the identity nor the affiliation of the speaker(s), nor that of any other participant, may be revealed.

We have identified a range of activities and workshop formats that can help enhance partnership building with universities. These activities largely focus on developing partnerships by providing opportunities to expose shared interests and through the facilitation of meaningful interaction across different topic areas/work streams. When thinking about who to invite, make sure you look wider than just science: look carefully beyond the usual science capabilities and explore the extent to which other disciplines, such as management schools, marketing, and media could be useful to your company.

- *Country- and region-based science symposiums.* Cross-academic network events that have entailed inviting all university partners in a region, plus other academic experts, and often focused on one or two key themes or topic areas. Useful in building the reputation of the company and in encouraging cross-partner collaborations. Small amounts of grant funding are often available to support these types of meeting.
- *WANT workshops.* Events focused on specific key issues that the company is seeking solution routes for. Often useful in helping better define the problem areas and flagging up solution routes and suitable expertise. These work well by including several academics from within just one institution, plus a range of your own company staff.
- *WANT speed-dating.* A simple and fun workshop format for matching researchers using the Science WANT template (Section 17). Can work with a large or small number of delegates; allow between two and five minutes for participants to introduce their research wants and specialisms before moving to the next person or table.
- *University visits.* Research managers and leaders from an institution can play a central role in co-ordinating visits to their institutions to allow a wider range of company staff to better understand the potential for engagement and the university's capabilities. Useful for business engagement – although be mindful of

managing expectations of the university partner about what can be achieved.

- *Selling the partnership to external funders.* Helping to raise awareness of the quality, capability, and reach of the partnership. This can often be done by weaving the key vision, mission, and impact of the partnership into external talks – building confidence in the partnership to help enable leverage.
- *Co-developing capability plans.* Working together in a workshop format to help articulate and define what capabilities will be needed by your company in the future. This format helps build buy-in to these problems from academic partners and helps to articulate the science problem in ways that resonate with them.
- *Partnership and strategic supplier.* Focused forums with company scientists, a university partner's academics, and representatives from strategic suppliers, to help define problems and associated solution routes. The aim is to create new insights and approaches from the combination of academic and industrial scientists. Be clear on the 'rules of engagement' (confidentiality, etc.) and take time to manage expectations at the outset of these sessions!

If there is a more substantive common innovation challenge, it may be worth investing in a more interactive workshop over a period of days involving 10–25 participants. These workshops often benefit from a highly multidisciplinary mix of participants, some active researchers, and other potential users of research outcomes. The objective is to drive lateral thinking and radical approaches to address research challenges.

28.
MEASURING SUCCESS

The projects you run and the partnerships you build with universities will ultimately need to deliver against the innovation and business agenda of your company. This section will help you take the temperature of both a project and the overall partnership, allowing you to find ways to improve their output and performance.

Looking first at individual projects, there are many possible dimensions on which to measure success and there is a balance to be struck. Single metrics of cost control, timeliness, or achieving a specification will fail to recognise the needs of all the stakeholders, whereas using ten separate measures removes any intuitive sense of progress. We favour a four-dimensional approach that we have adapted from work in the 1990s (Shenhar et al. 1997). It recognises that the relative importance of different factors changes over time. While a project is in progress, the efficiency of the programme in terms of cost and time will always be front of mind. As the project moves through to completion, it is the impact for the partner or customer that becomes most important – are they happy and do they think it was a success? After this, it is possible to assess the impact for the core business itself and then, sometime after the project has ended, the potential future benefits will become apparent – has the project created new opportunities and capabilities?

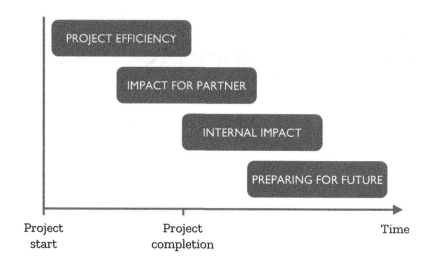

Figure 9: The changing dimensions of project success over time.

This model is illustrated in Figure 9. The four dimensions of project success change over the lifetime of the project. At the start of the project, all the attention of the project team needs to be on efficiency: getting the project started, putting in place team structures, securing technical resources, and creating simple and effective communications channels. As the project progresses, and new insights and results are created and shared, the project leadership can take some time to consider the impact the project is having on the project partner. At the end of the project, attention can turn to the impacts the project has had internally within the lead organisation, and eventually thinking about future opportunities based on the outcomes of this project.

In the assessment of how well a project has prepared you for the future, you move into the realm of assessing the effectiveness of the wider strategic partnership. This will help you reflect on the balance of achievements (i.e. outputs, outcomes, and impact) against the resources that have been invested, and support evaluations that help improve the quality of the partnership itself. The challenge that a company has when it tries to assess its strategic partnership with universities is that, by their nature, these partnerships are a long way from delivering market value. It can therefore be difficult to judge the value of the partnership on this type of output. It is very tricky to trace back and attribute to the root science or insight that enabled a resulting innovation because of the lengthy and complex processes that sit behind getting a product to market. Focusing only on 'benefits realisation' in terms of market impact will undervalue the role played by universities and their contribution – and is unhelpful in terms of monitoring the ongoing development of the relationship. Other indicators of success (and failure!) are therefore needed to understand how well the relationship is working and the trajectory a partnership is on. An important lens for viewing the relationship and its development is the idea of social capital, which we explained in detail in Section 22. The dimensions of social capital described in Table 12 are a useful means to evaluate the overall trajectory of a partnership.

The authors have been active in building strategic partnerships with academic institutions for decades. It is hard to make sweeping generalisations about the success factors involved in these partnerships, but one thing has become very clear: *no two company–university partnerships are the same.* Each partnership has grown organically out of specific project needs, specific scientific capability and funding opportunities, and the most pressing business priorities of a particular company or business unit. All partnerships are rooted to some extent in particular geographies, or in specific cross-geography networks. Each partnership has different strengths and weaknesses, and their uniqueness is part of how they bring value to both a company and the academic partners.

The following framework may be useful for you to reflect on the current state of the partnerships that you are actively working in. The model, which is presented on the following pages, can be used to address new opportunities for a partnership as well as demonstrating success.

As is true of assessing individual projects, the simplest and most direct way is to ask your partner how they think things are going. The model gives a more formal method of developing conversations with staff within your own department and university staff to reflect on the status of the partnership and identify areas for development.

METRIC	UNDERDEVELOPED RELATIONSHIP
Leadership	No shared vision of the future. Limited or basic governance arrangements for the partnership. Sporadic projects unsupported by service-level agreements. Scientific challenges poorly understood or not articulated.
Strategy	Infrequent communication between partners limited to transactions and formal arrangements. Absence of known success stories. Little or no promotion of collaboration.
Portfolio	No shared or joint agreements in place. Limited understanding of technical processes. IP, publishing, terms and conditions negotiated on a case-by-case basis. Relationships are highly dependent on key people.
Research	Little understanding of each other's culture and values. Limited shared language or knowledge of the challenges each organisation is facing.
Communication	Only reactive opportunity responses limited to bilateral agreements.

Table 17: Evaluating underdeveloped relationships.

This can help you to recognise where you are and build momentum. This framework alone will not provide you with a sufficiently robust evaluation of the partnership, but it is a handy tool to generate some useful insight in a short space of time.

METRIC	SUCCESSFUL STRATEGIC PARTNERSHIP
Leadership	Long-term, shared vision articulated as the relationship develops. A joint statement of endeavour has been agreed. Decision makers and relationship leads identified. Working across all areas in the interactions quadrant to maximise capabilities.
Strategy	Scientific challenges are well understood. University and company both understand opportunities for collaboration.
Portfolio	Differences of opinion are openly articulated and resolved. Frequent informal conversations and exchanges take place.
Research	Key success stories are captured, shared, and understood.
Communication	The collaboration is publicly recognised and celebrated. Joint statements have been announced. Success stories are readily shared with the press and online platforms.

Table 18: Evaluating successful strategic partnerships.

If you want to take it further, you may consider bringing in some additional evaluation expertise to help you gain deeper insight. This could either be another company R&D person who has the right skills and experience, or an external consultant. Factors that will influence your choice will include your available budget, specialist skills, domain expertise, flexibility, and independence. Whichever approach you go for, there are some key principles to take into account when conducting an effective evaluation.

- *Involve partners throughout the process.* The key stakeholders in the company and your partners should be consulted when trying to set the scope of an evaluation. The framework in Table 18 is only a starting point.
- *Don't evaluate too early.* Although the evaluation framework may be clear from the beginning, nobody will thank you for trying to evaluate this before there is real experience of how things are going.
- *Provide a means for genuine feedback.* Sometimes close partners will feel inhibited about being critical. Online surveys and anonymised questionnaires and interviews should be used sparingly, but are often a source of great specific feedback.

This framework needs to be considered in the context of the rest of this playbook. The headings used here are simply to bring the attention of your company and the partner to some key areas required for success. There is no quantitative scale for any of these factors, so we would suggest you don't try to scale them. However, it is very productive to craft short, qualitative statements about the current state of the partnership that can then be evaluated.

29.
CLOSING WORDS

We hope the guidance, tools, and resources provided here will help you to understand the strategic value that can be created by working with universities, and support you on your journey to nurture more effective partnerships – anything from high-quality ad hoc projects, to more sustained and longer-term strategic collaborations.

In addition to the material we present here, our website (www. upp-book.com) has plenty of additional material for those who want to apply the tools we have described.

While the tools presented here and on our website have all been tested and are proven to work, there is also room to improve them, and we invite you to do so! Good luck and enjoy the journey!

REFERENCES

Bill & Melinda Gates Foundation, www.gatesfoundation.org/.

Boschma, R.A., 'Proximity and Innovation: A Critical Assessment', *Regional Studies*, 39 (2005), 61–74.

Brannan, C.F., then the Secretary of Agriculture, USA, on an NBC broadcast on 3 April 1949.

Burns, J.M., *Leadership* (New York: Harper & Row, 1978).

Carlsson, B., and R. Stankiewicz, 'On the Nature, Function and Composition of Technological Systems', *Journal of Evolutionary Economics*, 1 (1991), 93–118.

Chatham House Rule, www.chathamhouse.org/chatham-house-rule.

DeMarco, T., and T. Lister, *Peopleware: Productive Projects and Teams* (New York: Dorset House, 1999).

Doz, Y.L., and G. Hamel, *Alliance Advantage: The Art of Creating Value Through Partnering* (Boston, MA: Harvard Business Review Press, 1998).

Fine, C.H., *Clockspeed* (London: Little, Brown, 1999).

Gigerenzer, G., *Simply Rational: Decision Making in the Real World* (Oxford: Oxford University Press, 2015).

Graeber, D., *The Utopia of Rules: On Technology, Stupidity, and the Secret Joys of Bureaucracy* (Brooklyn, NY/London: Melville House, 2015).

Haldane, H., and V. Madouros, 'The Dog and the Frisbee', *Proceedings – Economic Policy Symposium – Jackson Hole* (2012), pp. 109–159.

Iansiti M., and R. Levien, 'Strategy as Ecology', *Harvard Business Review*, March (2004).

Nahapiet, J., and S. Ghoshal, 'Social Capital, Intellectual Capital, and the Organizational Advantage', *Academy of Management Review*, 23 (1998), 242–266.

NASA (1974), www.nasa.gov/directorates/heo/scan/engineering/technology/txt_accordion1.html.

Paine, L., 'Sustainability in the Boardroom', *Harvard Business Review*, July–August (2014).

Pronin, E., 'How We See Ourselves and How We See Others', *Science*, 30 (2008), 1177–1180.

QS World University Rankings, www.topuniversities.com/university-rankings.

Shenhar, A.J., and others, 'Mapping the Dimensions of Project Success', *Project Management Journal*, 28 (1997), 5–13.

Simon, H.A., *Administrative Behavior: A Study of Decision-Making Processes in Administrative Organization* (New York/London: Macmillan, 1947).

Times Higher Education University rankings, www.timeshighereducation.com/world-university-rankings.

UK Research & Innovation (UKRI), www.ukri.org/innovation/excellence-with-impact/.

VSNU (2014), 'The Standard Evaluation Protocol', https://rio.jrc.ec.europa.eu/en/library/standard-evaluation-protocol-2015-2021.

Weber, M., *Economy and Society*, ed. by Guenther Roth and Claus Wittich (Berkeley: University of California Press, 1978/1922).

FURTHER READING

Ashby, D., and C. Jensen, *APIs for Dummies* (Hoboken, NJ: John Wiley & Sons, 2018).

Frølund, L., and others, 'Developing Successful Strategic Partnerships with Universities', *MIT Sloan Management Review*, 59 (2018), 71–79.

Horner, S., and B. Giordano, '"Made in Liverpool": Exploring the Contribution of a University–Industry Research Partnership to Innovation and Entrepreneurship', in *Entrepreneurship, Universities & Resources Frontiers in European Entrepreneurship Research*, ed. by U. Hytti and others (Cheltenham, UK: Edward Elgar, 2016), pp. 168–193.

Perkmann, M., 'University–Industry Relations', in *Concise Guide to Entrepreneurship, Technology and Innovation*, ed. by D.B. Audretsch and others (Cheltenham, UK: Edward Elgar, 2015), pp. 227–233.

Perkmann, M., and A. Salter, 'How to Create Productive Partnerships with Universities', *MIT Sloan Management Review*, 53 (2012), 4.

Perkmann, M., and others, 'Academic Engagement and Commercialisation: A Review of the Literature on University–Industry Relations', *Research Policy*, 42 (2013), 423–442.

ACKNOWLEDGEMENTS

This book could not have been written and published without the generous and enthusiastic support of Dr Jonathan Hague, the VP Science & Technology for Home Care R&D, Unilever.

Much of the base material was originally prepared for an internal Unilever R&D workshop that was held in Port Sunlight, UK, in December 2016. The experiences and insights of the workshop participants and their external partners made the original playbook possible: Amitava Pramamik, Eddie Pelan, Gail Jenkins, Guoping Lian, Janette Jones, Mark Berry, Mike Butler, Ian Stott, Massimo Noro, Nitin Deshpande, Samiran Mahapatra, Scott Singleton, Paul Pudney, Simeon Stoyanov, Nancy Gu, Gautam Chatterjee, Jon Hague, Linda Edwards, Rimma Mitelman, Mike Shaw, Sam Samaras, with support from Chris Thompson and Vanessa Bailey (Viadynamics Ltd). The copy editing of the first edition of this book was supported by David Owen (Gurukula Ltd).

ACKNOWLEDGEMENTS

INDEX

Printed and bound by CPI Group (UK) Ltd, Croydon, CR0 4YY

13/04/2025

14656559-0006